ALSO BY DAVID MARANISS

First in His Class: A Biography of Bill Clinton

"Tell Newt to Shut Up!"
(with Michael Weisskopf)

THE
CLINTON
ENIGMA

A Four-and-a-Half-Minute Speech

Reveals This President's Entire Life

DAVID MARANISS

SIMON & SCHUSTER

SIMON & SCHUSTER
Rockefeller Center
1230 Avenue of the Americas
New York, NY 10020

SIMON & SCHUSTER and colophon are registered trademarks
of Simon & Schuster Inc.

Designed by Edith Fowler

Manufactured in the United States of America

1 3 5 7 9 10 8 6 4 2

Library of Congress Cataloging-in-Publication Data is available.

ISBN 0-684-86296-4

PART ONE

Waiting for Clinton

ONE

I SUPPOSE it had to come to this, I thought to myself as I sat in the darkness of the NBC studio nook in New York, waiting for the familiar image of Bill Clinton to appear on the monitor. In a few minutes, Clinton would deliver a televised address to the nation concerning his extramarital sex life, a subject that no president before him had been compelled to discuss in public. It was obvious that he dreaded giving this speech, but circumstances had forced him into it; he thought his career was on the line. As his biographer, I would be asked to try to explain him, both what his words meant and why he had reached such an unfortunate moment. I had spent six years studying Clinton, but emotionally I had now moved beyond him, onto the subject of my next biography, Vince Lombardi, the old Green Bay Packers coach, a resolute symbol of the past who seemed to be the antithesis of the prodigal young president. It was nonetheless still impossible to escape Clinton professionally; he kept doing things that yanked me as a reporter back into his world.

Another thought troubled me more. I liked to believe, perhaps naively, that the freest of all things was the human will, that we can learn and respond and change. Clinton's life kept threatening that assumption. He was a protean character who constantly adapted to his environment, an intelligent man with an extraordinary memory for names and faces and events and an uncommon ability to assemble facts and synthesize arguments, yet at a deeper level he seemed incapable of learning and changing. He was like General George Armstrong Custer as described by biographer Evan Connell before the Battle of Little Bighorn, his fate determined by the immutability of his character, reacting predictably to the same stimuli again and again and again.

As I waited for Clinton to deliver his August 17 apologia for having some form of sex with the young intern, Monica Lewinsky, and lying about it, my mind drifted back to the first time I had interviewed him, more than six years earlier. The date was January 20, 1992, exactly one year before his first inauguration. We were gliding through the night in the backseat of a dark blue Buick taking him from Annapolis to the Washington suburbs. Questions about his sexual behavior had already become part of the early campaign discussion that year. At a debate of the Democratic presidential candidates in New Hampshire, he had been asked about the sexual innuendo that surrounded him, and he had responded that he did not think there was reason for anyone to expect embarrassing stories to emerge about his sex life. After covering Gary Hart in 1984 and writing about Hart's self-implosion on issues of sex in 1987, I found Clinton's answer curiously imprecise. Reconfiguring the question in the context of Hart's political demise, I asked Clinton about it again during my interview with him for a profile I was writing for *The Washington Post*: "Do you understand how many millions of people you might let down if you won the nomination and then were confronted with stories like those that hounded Hart out of the race?"

Clinton did not look at me when he answered, nor did he respond directly to the question. He began to talk, then took a phone call from Jesse Jackson on his cell phone, all uh-huhs and southern whispers, then got off the phone and sarcastically disparaged Jackson as a pest, then returned to what amounted to a long diversion, saying that he didn't want to get into Gary Hart, but that Hart's situation was an entirely different matter from his own. The fact that he would not engage the larger question of consequences left me feeling uneasy about him, though in other ways I found his life's story colorful and intriguing. A few days later, the Gennifer Flowers story broke.

And now here we were, all these years later, with Clinton a second-term president fighting to save his job in the face of a sex scandal (and coincidentally turning to that same Reverend Jackson for family counseling)—and with that first question I asked him in the back of the dark sedan still hovering out there, unanswered. It is the reason why I never thought of his sexual behavior as exclusively a privacy issue, nor merely as a matter of sex. It seemed to me a matter of narcissism, arrogance, stupidity, and cynicism. If he knew from the beginning that his enemies were out to get him, as he and his wife, Hillary Rodham Clinton, have so often claimed, then he also knew where he was most vulnerable to attack. That was the reality, and it transcended whatever he or anyone else thought about the relevance of a public official's private life or the obsessively invasive nature of his prosecutorial adversary. I always thought that he and his supporters had strong arguments against the special prosecutor and that in the end the process might be remembered as much as the substance of Clinton's wrongdoing. I also oppose the death penalty, and believe the issue of capital punishment is far larger than any individual case, but that does not excuse the murderer or make it less important to remove him from society or to understand why he murders and to deplore the consequences of his act—even when police use questionable means to catch him.

Clinton is a dissembler, far from a murderer, despite the fantastical tales of his wildest enemies, so the analogy is not precise, but the point is much the same. The writer Francine du Plessix Gray, biographer of the Marquis de Sade, told me that she suspected that Clinton, like Sade, was only excited by risk and recklessness. In any event, the reality that Clinton never seemed willing to deal with was that his risk was not his alone; that his actions had consequences not just for himself and his family and friends, but also for millions of people, some who believed in him, some who cared about his policies, some who despised his enemies and did not want them to prevail, some who just wanted to think positively about human nature.

TWO

MEMORIES OF OTHER ENCOUNTERS with Clinton came back to me as I waited in the studio for him to deliver his fateful speech. More accurately, they were near encounters. While researching articles for the *Post* on the forces that shaped his life and career, I had talked with him at length seven times during the 1992 campaign, but starting the day he won the election, the same day that I decided to write his biography, he declined all of my interview requests. I never received a firm no, just indications from one of his White House aides, usually Dee Dee Myers or George Stephanopoulos, sometimes his former chief of staff in Arkansas, Betsey Wright, that he wanted another memo about it, or was still thinking about it, or most likely would not do it but might change his mind later. At one point, I received word through Mrs. Clinton that he was advised not to talk to me by one of his personal lawyers, who said it might detract from his presidential memoirs, a notion I found preposterous.

Clinton had a perfect right to reject the interview requests. I never felt that he was obligated to talk to me simply because I was writing a book about his life. I was brought up with a deep regard for civil liberties and believe that the right of someone to remain silent is as important as the right for someone to speak freely. But his rebuffs were revealing; he seemed far less comfortable talking about his past with someone who had studied it than discussing the future—which could only be imagined—with anyone.

In the days before *First in His Class* was published in March 1995, Clinton revealed more of himself to me through three encounters with emissaries. The first involved David Kendall, one of his personal lawyers, who called me one morning and invited me to join him at his law offices at Williams & Connolly for what he defined as a casual working lunch. He ushered me into a strange little room that felt like a cross between a luxurious private dining chamber and an interrogation cell, airless, closeted, with fine china. An elegant meal was served between his firm but polite queries. He understood that my biography of Clinton was coming out shortly, Kendall said, and he wanted to do me the favor of making sure that no grievous errors were in it concerning the Whitewater investigation. It was possible that he had obtained an advance review copy of the book—they were floating around Washington—but he never indicated so. Nor did I tell him what was in the biography. I already had heard that he was among the Clinton associates encouraging another author to write a book that they hoped would present the Whitewater controversy from their perspective. I did tell him that my book was not about Whitewater and that I wished Clinton would talk to me himself.

Not long afterward, I received a call from Mike McCurry, who was one day away from officially taking over as the president's new press secretary. I had known McCurry since his undergraduate years at Princeton University in the mid-1970s, when I worked at the nearby *Trenton Times*, covering Princeton, and he was the paper's campus stringer. He was smart and witty with a charming manner, though he was more graceful verbally than on the printed page, so it did not surprise me that he had taken the other road, choosing the life of a political publicist. I had seen him only a few times over the years, most recently in New Hampshire in 1992, when he was working for another Democratic presidential hopeful, Senator Bob Kerrey of Nebraska; we had stumbled into each other near the gift shop at the Sheraton Wayfarer one morning and he had mumbled conspiratorially that he thought the sex-plagued governor of Arkansas was going straight down the tubes.

Now McCurry was on the telephone the night before his first official day in the White House. "Hey, David," he began, "I got a call from the president at two o'clock last night and he said to me, 'Find out why I never talked to Maraniss for his book.' I'm coming in cold to all this, so I thought maybe you could help me understand. Why didn't he talk to you for your book?"

Give me a break, I thought. All the memos I'd drafted to the White House explaining the methodology of my biography, how I was interviewing hundreds of people, all on the record, gathering documents and letters, determined to write neither a hatchet job nor hagiography but a fair study of Clinton and his generational cohorts. All the times I had heard indirectly about Clinton debriefing people I had interviewed, trying to find out what questions I had asked and what I knew. All the times I had called the White House renewing my interview request after reading about how he had talked to some other reporter while claiming that he was too preoccupied with the presidency to deal with me. And now he wanted McCurry to find out for him why he hadn't talked to me?

"Mike," I said, "when you get the answer to that question, you'll find out everything you need to know about your new boss." Clinton didn't talk to me because he didn't want to talk to me. Now maybe he wished that he had, so he was conveniently denying that it was his choice all along. I wished McCurry good luck.

Just before the biography's release, a third peculiar call came, this one from Betsey Wright. I had interviewed Wright many times for the book and considered her relationship with Clinton invaluable to my understanding of him. She was a troubled soul, alternately depressed and overflowing with enthusiasm, sometimes brilliant, other times out of her element in national politics. She seemed to represent all the contradictions that people who really knew Clinton carried with them. She loved him and hated him. She had a right to hate him, he had placed her in so many difficult situations over the years, but it was a fine line and she did not want others to hate him. At the same time that she was protecting him from what she once famously called "bimbo eruptions," she was telling me about her worst times with him. One of those times came in the summer of 1987, a few months after Gary Hart was forced out of the presidential race. Clinton had invited his friends down to Little Rock and rented a hotel conference room with the intention of announcing for president himself, backing out only at the last minute, Wright said, after she had confronted him with a list of women who might be problematic for him.

When I had finished writing the biography, I met with Wright in Washington, where she was working as a lobbyist, and I read to her every scene in the book in which she appeared. Although the meeting was uncomfortable, we had parted on solid terms with an understanding that she stood by what she had told me. But now, as the book was on the verge of release, she dialed my telephone number at work late at night and left a long message on the tape of my answering machine. Bill, as she still called him, had heard some stories about what was in the book and was furious about the description of the scene in 1987 and a few other incidents involving his sex life. He was pressuring her to deny the accounts. The White House was calling her a traitor, she said. Everyone over there was mad at her. She added that she regretted that she had told me so much, she wished she hadn't, but she had, and it was the truth, and she didn't know what to do now. I heard the message the next morning when I came into the *Post* and realized that she had purposely placed the call at a time when I would not be there so it could serve as a record no matter what happened. I immediately replayed the tape for the *Post*'s executive editor, Leonard Downie. It was evidence of her real feelings in case the pressure on her to change her story increased.

It did. Within twenty-four hours, Wright had issued a variation of the nondenial denial, saying that I had apparently misinterpreted what she had said to me in the interviews. She called me in an apologetic tone before she released the statement and said it was something that she had to do. Her statement was included in a front-page story in the *Post* that went over the highlights of the book, including the 1987 scene between Wright and Clinton. I was besieged with calls from newspapers, television networks, and radio stations around the country and the world on the morning that the *Post* article about the book appeared.

The first call came before 6:30 A.M. from a reporter for the *New Delhi Times*, inquiring about "Bill Clinton's sex life." The second came from a radio reporter in Seattle who left a message saying she wanted to talk to me about "Bill Clinton and Betsey Wright and their sex life." It went on from there, more than seventy calls in one morning, all about Clinton and sex. If it is possible to be confused but not surprised at the same time, that is how I felt that day. I had spent three years and conducted hundreds of interviews for the very purpose of examining Clinton's life in its full complexity, to get beyond the stereotypes of the moment, and now the result of all that labor, the biography, was out, and it was being reduced to a few paragraphs about sex. I should have expected this reaction. Clinton's first national image was formed amid the Gennifer Flowers controversy, and sex had become a metaphor for his character ever since. But while I understood the focus on the few sex scenes in the book, it still depressed me. I recoiled, refusing to do interviews that day or the next. The story died quickly.

THREE

ONCE, IN 1981, when he was out of government briefly, having been defeated as governor of Arkansas after only one two-year term, Clinton appeared as a guest lecturer at a political literature course at the University of Arkansas in Fayetteville. He analyzed some of the more complex and compelling political characters in literature, including Willie Stark, the corrupt southern governor in Robert Penn Warren's *All the King's Men*. He also discussed several biographies that had helped shape his perspective, including ones of Lincoln, Hitler, and Churchill. In all political leaders, Clinton told the class, there was a struggle between darkness and light. He mentioned the darkness of insecurity, depression, and family disorder. In great leaders, he said, the light overcame the darkness, but it was always a struggle.

This observation is obvious, but it stuck with me throughout my study of Clinton. I tend to be forgiving, interested in finding light as well as darkness; the struggle between those two forces is what fascinates me, the humanity in any person, especially one who appears to have the makings of an underdog.

It was not difficult to find the darker corners of Clinton's life. He could be deceptive, and he came from a family in which lying and philandering were routine, two traits that he apparently had not overcome. As he grew older, the more tension he felt between idealism and ambition, the more he gave in to his ambition, sometimes at the expense of friends and causes that he had once

believed in. I could also see his sources of light. He was a father-
less son who came out of the depths of provincial southwestern
Arkansas and never seemed ashamed of his roots. Many people
who have dismissed him as a calculating phony are far more in-
vented creatures and less connected to their pasts than he has always been. I was struck by the friends he seemed to have made
over the years, many of them people I greatly admired, such as
Taylor Branch, the chronicler of the civil rights era, or others who
were lovable and utterly without guile, such as his Hot Springs
childhood pal David Leopoulos and Georgetown roommate Tom
Campbell. He seemed to have multiple personalities, some re-
deeming. The forces of light often prevailed when he dealt with
African Americans and other minorities. When he was a young
law professor at the University of Arkansas, he tutored the first
wave of black students at the law school, who before he arrived
had felt alienated, without mentors. It was his intense interest in
their lives, many of them said later, that made it possible for them
to survive and get their law degrees. They called him "Wonder
Boy."

Clinton's ability to empathize with others, his desire to become a peacemaker and bring diverse groups together, always
struck me as the better part of his character. It was, to me, the first
necessary ingredient of any good leader, and something that most
American politicians seemed to lack. I also came to think of his
indomitable nature as a mostly positive trait; his refusal to give up
and to find a way out of whatever predicament he found himself
in, usually a mess of his own making, in some sense represented
to me man's eternal struggle to persist in spite of his imperfec-
tions.

When *First in His Class* was published, Clinton was at the
lowest point of his career since his defeat as governor in 1980. He
had lost the major initiative of his first term, health care reform,
and with it control of Congress in the 1994 elections. Newt Gingrich was suddenly dominant in Washington, and Clinton seemed
diminished if not irrelevant. Don Graham, the publisher of the
Post, sarcastic as he is gracious, summed up the general feeling
about my biography by muttering, "Nice timing, Maraniss." The
conventional wisdom was that Clinton was not worth worrying
about, a goner, one term and out. I predicted that Clinton would
persevere and come back, and that he would do it the same way

that he had in Arkansas, by following the advice of consultant Dick Morris, who had masterminded his earlier resurrection but was then virtually unknown in Washington. He would move to the political center and wait for his enemies to overplay their hand. When it happened precisely that way, I thought to myself, Can life really be that repetitive and predictable? Clinton was.

FOUR

SOME OF IT can be explained by my bias for the underdog again, but I usually find Clinton least likable when he is riding high. The symbolic expression of that arrogance came last spring when he was in Africa and received word that the Paula Jones case had been dismissed, and the cameras that evening found him up in his lighted hotel room, champing on an unlit cigar, pounding joyously on a drum. When I see him like that, only one thought enters my mind: Trouble is on the way. It is as though he has a neon sign flashing on his forehead: Hubris. Hubris. Hubris. Clinton was riding high for most of 1996, after the Republicans had shut down the government and handed him back his presidency, and done him the further favor of running old Bob Dole against him, allowing him to frame the election as a choice between the twenty-first and nineteenth centuries.

I covered that election for the *Post* and submitted numerous requests to Mike McCurry for interviews with the president. Clinton had not talked to me since the book came out. I knew that many of his friends and associates regarded it as fair and accurate, but that he had hated the half of it that was critical of him and that had revealed the patterns of his duplicity. Dick Morris, who had talked to me extensively for the biography and was then running the reelection campaign, told me that Clinton would never deal with me for two reasons: first, I knew him too well, and it made him uncomfortable; and, second, the few portions of the book that examined his sex life upset the first lady so much that she had turned "frosty" on the president for several weeks and had refused to talk to him or sleep in the same bedroom with him in the White House residence.

This struck me as peculiar. What I wrote about Clinton's sexual behavior was so mild compared with the stories that Arkansas state troopers had told the *Los Angeles Times* and the *American Spectator*, and Mrs. Clinton had been dealing with her husband's waywardness for more than two decades—why would my book trigger such a fierce reaction? The answer, as it came back to me from White House aides, was revealing then, and had echoes in her response to the Lewinsky scandal two years later. When it came to Clinton and sex, she knew but she didn't want to know. Unless confronted directly by evidence that she accepted and could not ignore, she redirected her attention and her anger at their shared enemies. She believed what I wrote, especially since some of it came not from their adversaries but from Betsey Wright. She did not yet consider me part of a right-wing conspiracy, though she was starting to develop a theory that *The Washington Post* was out to get her and the president.

Clinton, in a winning mood, gave interviews to all the major news organizations during the week before his triumphant train ride to Chicago in August 1996, where he would accept his party's nomination for a second term. The *Post* was granted an interview, and three reporters were to take part in it: John Harris, the White House correspondent; Dan Balz, the chief political correspondent; and me, the Clinton biographer. I was writing a piece examining how he had come back from the depths of 1994. A few hours before the scheduled appointment at the White House, as I was sitting at my desk preparing questions, the phone rang and it was McCurry on the line. Was I really planning to participate in the interview? he asked. Yes, of course, he already knew that. "Well," he said, "it would be better if you didn't come. If you're there, it might blow up the interview." McCurry never said it directly, but the implication was that the president would not talk to the *Post* if I was there. That meant that Clinton had learned I was coming and had indicated to his staff that he did not like it. I told my editors on the national staff, Karen DeYoung, Bill Hamilton, and Maralee Schwartz, and we decided that this was not worth taking a principled stand over; Balz and Harris could go without me.

The truth is that I had no intention of asking Clinton uncomfortable questions about his private life, and in fact never was
particularly interested in doing so. I already knew that he was a
master at ignoring or filibustering questions that he found dis-
comforting. In any case, when the *Post* delegation entered the
Oval Office that afternoon, Clinton noticed that it consisted only
of Harris and Balz. "Where's David?" he asked, with the wistful
tone of someone missing a long-lost friend. "I haven't seen him in
a long time."

The next month, I put in another request for an interview
with Clinton, this one for a *Washington Post Magazine* story I was
preparing on Dole and Clinton, "The Old Man and the Kid." I
traveled with the White House press corps following the president
on a campaign swing from Chicago to the Grand Canyon to Las
Vegas and up to Washington State, where the Clintons and Gores
launched another of their bus trips. On the second day, McCurry
told me that Clinton and Hillary had spotted me in the crowd a
few times and had wondered aloud why I was there. On the third
day, he informed me that the Clinton entourage was unhappy
with a letter from the campaign trail I had written for the *Post* in
which I had described Clinton on a roll as a man with a voracious
and barely restrained appetite, wanting more crowds, more
speeches, more hands to shake, more programs to promise, more
of everything. Harold Ickes, the deputy chief of staff, complained
that I was using appetite as a code word for sex. Not really, but an
interestingly defensive perspective.

Near the end of the trip, McCurry came up to me with
promising news: I would finally get the Clinton interview. There
would be a long flight back to Washington, D.C., interrupted
only by a brief stop in South Dakota, and for the second leg of that
journey, he said, they would take me off the press plane and put
me in the back of *Air Force One*. "It's going to be a Maraniss moment," he said, smiling wryly. So I traipsed off the press plane in
Sioux Falls and found a seat with the small press pool that ac-
companies the president in his partitioned jumbo jet. Thirty minutes into the flight, McCurry came back and found me. "Follow
me," he said, leading me to an empty quarter in the midsection of
the plane that looked like a little classroom. "Look, the president's
tired," McCurry said. "He's not going to talk to you. He's not in

the mood to entertain your questions about the condition of his soul. What you are interested in has nothing to do with this campaign. He's got an election to win."

We landed in Washington late that night, and on the tarmac at Andrews Air Force Base, as I was hauling my suitcase to the terminal, McCurry came over to me one last time. "After the election," he said, "you'll get the very first interview after the election. Promise." Then he explained that his boss was as difficult for him to deal with as he was for me, and he turned his baseball cap around with the brim facing backward, Junior Griffey style, and ran across the runway to *Marine One* for a chopper ride through the darkness to the White House.

I did not get the first Clinton interview after the election. That went to David Brinkley of ABC News, who had eased the way for his scoop by thoroughly trashing the president as a phony a few days earlier. After that, McCurry stopped answering my faxes, and I persuaded my wife to move out to Green Bay, Wisconsin, with me for the winter so that I could begin my biography of Vince Lombardi, whom I did not have to worry about avoiding me since he was dead.

One final memory of my dealings with Clinton came back to me as I waited for him to deliver his apology speech, an appropriate little coda to my experiences with him. In May 1997, the president and I found ourselves on the same dais at a luncheon meeting of the American Society of Newspaper Editors. He was the guest speaker; I was among the award winners. Clinton was on crutches, hobbling from his late-night stumble down golfer Greg Norman's stairs. He entered the room from the other side and worked his way only halfway down the dais to the podium before he gave his speech. When it was over, he worked the other side, my side. My mind raced. So much that I knew, so many questions I wanted to ask. But of course I could think of nothing to say.

"Long time," I muttered.

"Hi, David," he said. "Congratulations on your award. Nice tie."

And then he was gone, hobbling on. Classic Clinton, I thought. My wife and father were in the audience, and I whispered down to them, "He said, 'Nice tie.'" Clinton worked the rope line, and when he reached my family, he stopped and chatted about his knee injury for several minutes. More classic Clinton. He won't talk to me but he'll wow my wife and father. Later, I heard that my dad's first words to him were "Nice tie."

In the summer of 1998, in New York, I was talking to George Stephanopoulos, who had left the White House and was struggling to finish a bittersweet memoir of his Clinton years, toiling away in his luxury apartment on Riverside Drive. He seemed surprised when I told him that my only encounter with Clinton since the book came out had been on the dais that day in May. As a fellow expert on Clinton lexicon, he offered up a definition for the president's "Nice tie" utterance. In that context, he said, it had another meaning. "What it meant was 'Fuck you,'" he explained. At that moment, I confess, I was secretly heartened by the recollection that my father, an old progressive, had unwittingly responded in kind.

PART TWO

Listening to Clinton

FIVE

TEN O'CLOCK MONDAY NIGHT, August 17: The camera zoomed in on Clinton in the Map Room, where earlier that day he had spent four hours being questioned by Kenneth Starr and deputies from the independent counsel's office. Now he was ready to speak to the nation. His image on the television monitor looked pinched, his face blurry, his features slightly distorted and misplaced, more like his late mother, the oddly exotic Virginia, than I had ever noticed before. His countenance seemed angry, frustrated at the least, the way I had imagined Virginia would look back when Billy was a boy in Hot Springs and she would come home to the tan brick ranch house on Scully Street after a long day at the hospital and slam her bulky purse down on the kitchen counter and exclaim, "You wouldn't believe what they did to me today!" All day long, reports had been seeping out of the White House that the president would not go gently into this strange night. He was raging, as was Hillary, for many different reasons—furious that after a quarter-century together their remarkable political partnership had been reduced to this. Clinton's peeved disposition fit a pattern that I had come to expect. He started to talk. His mouth was tense and dry, all cotton; the uncomfortable sound of swallow and purse after every sentence in a desperate search for saliva.

*Good evening. This afternoon in this room, from this chair, I testi-
fied before the office of independent counsel and a grand jury. I answered their questions truthfully, including questions about my
private life, questions no American citizen would ever want to answer.*

*Still I must take complete responsibility for all my actions,
both public and private. And that is why I am speaking to you
tonight.*

*As you know, in a deposition in January, I was asked questions
about my relationship with Monica Lewinsky. While my answers
were legally accurate, I did not volunteer information. Indeed I did
have a relationship with Miss Lewinsky that was not appropriate.
In fact it was wrong.*

*It constituted a critical lapse in judgment and a personal fail-
ure on my part for which I am solely and completely responsible.*

*But I told the grand jury today, and I say to you now, that at
no time did I ask anyone to lie, to hide or destroy evidence, or to take
any other unlawful action.*

*I know that my public comments and my silence about this
matter gave a false impression. I misled people. Including even my
wife. I deeply regret that.*

*I can only tell you I was motivated by many factors. First, by a
desire to protect myself from the embarrassment of my own conduct.
I was also very concerned about protecting my family. The fact that
these questions were being asked in a politically inspired lawsuit
which has since been dismissed was a consideration too.*

*In addition, I had real and serious concerns about an inde-
pendent counsel investigation that began with private business
dealings twenty years ago—dealings, I might add, about which an
independent federal agency found no evidence of any wrongdoing
by me or my wife over two years ago.*

*The independent counsel investigation moved on to my staff
and friends. Then into my private life. And now the investigation itself is under investigation. This has gone on too long, cost too much,
and hurt too many innocent people.*

*Now this matter is between me, the two people I love most, my
wife and our daughter, and our God. I must put it right. And I am
prepared to do whatever it takes to do so.*

*Nothing is more important to me personally, but it is private.
And I intend to reclaim my family life for my family. It's nobody's*

*business but ours. Even presidents have private lives. It is time to
stop the pursuit of personal destruction and the prying into private
lives and get on with our national life.*

*Our country has been distracted by this matter for too long,
and I take responsibility for my part in all of this. That is all I can
do. Now it is time, in fact it is past time, to move on. We have important work to do, real opportunities to seize, real problems to
solve, real security matters to face.*

*And so tonight I ask you to turn away from the spectacle of the
past seven months, to repair the fabric of our national discourse and
to return our attention to all the challenges and all the promise of
the next American century. Thank you for watching and good
night.*

The speech took four and a half minutes to deliver and was
composed of 543 words, none particularly memorable. The public liked it more than the political elite, a divide over Clinton that
has been apparent for years, and one that had become especially
obvious throughout the first seven months of the Lewinsky sex
scandal. Political insiders disparaged it as a blown chance. MEA
NOT SO CULPA read one editorial headline. No apology to his supporters, nor to his staff, nor to Monica, nor to the country. Words
of rationalization to explain himself. Another attempt at lawyerly
evasion. And, most of all, an attack on Ken Starr. The tone
changed not quite halfway through, near the end of the seventh
paragraph, and never returned to its earlier form; the focus moved
away from Clinton and toward Starr, away from the past and
toward the future. None of the words surprised me. I had heard
them all before, though never at one time in one speech. As I listened to the president that night, the thought struck me that this
uneasy little address, born of necessity, shaped for survival, delivered with stubborn persistence, argumentative to the last, brush-
ing off history, clinging to hope, ringing with the urge to start over
and move forward, hated by the elite, grudgingly accepted by
the public, somehow reverberated with all the qualities of Bill
Clinton's melodramatic political life. It was also, in a sense, the
opening speech of what might be called Bill Clinton's third presidential campaign.

SIX

CLINTON HAD RECEIVED much unsolicited advice to follow the *mea culpa* route to survival. Senator Orrin Hatch of Utah, the self-styled moral arbiter for the Republicans, his starched collar riding ever higher up his righteous nape, had been suggesting that the odds against the president's impeachment would be set in direct proportion to the sincerity of his public repentance. Former aides Morris, Stephanopoulos, and Leon Panetta, who had long suspected that their old boss was not telling the truth, had asserted that the surest way for Clinton to save his presidency was to make a full public confession and seek forgiveness. Morris, who had consoled Clinton with perhaps the most honest three words spoken to the president after the story broke in January—"You poor bastard," he said sympathetically, having been felled by a sex scandal himself two years earlier—even conducted a poll to see how an apology might play. It seemed that everyone had an idea about what the speech should say. Consultants faxed in drafts that somehow found their way to news bureaus around Washington; former speechwriters phoned in suggestions; pundits distributed mock texts as the bare minimum level of groveling that Clinton should undertake; even novelists at summer dinner parties on Long Island conjured up the words that they would utter if they were in the president's predicament.

The idea of absolution was not alien to Clinton. Redemption is one of the most powerful themes of his Southern Baptist theology. Every day to him was a new day, fresh and free; he awoke with a feeling that John Updike once likened to a clean, clear scoreboard on a Saturday morning before the big game. But seeking forgiveness was one thing, saying he was sorry was quite another. There had always been a countervailing instinct in Clinton not to apologize unless he had no other choice, and then to do it reluctantly or halfheartedly. His historic tendency was to think that his problems were someone else's fault, sometimes with reason, often not.

The only true Clinton *mea culpa* had come when he was trying to resurrect his career after losing the Arkansas governorship in 1980, at age thirty-four, rendered the youngest ex-governor in American history. His instincts then were to find out everything he could about what had gone wrong, and to change his approach if necessary, but not to apologize. He relented only when consultant Morris, who had been plotting Clinton's comeback, persuaded him that an abject apology was the only strategy that would work. Morris had discovered in his surveys of Arkansas voters that the public had a paternal attitude toward Clinton, thinking of him as a member of the family, their precocious, wayward, prodigal son, whom they had voted against because they wanted to teach him a lesson for the way he had behaved during his first term — raising taxes, appearing arrogant — but whom they did not intend to send into permanent and premature exile.

From that, Morris crafted a parable of forgiveness, drawing on Christian theology. "You have to recognize your sins, confess them, and promise to sin no more and then sin no more," Morris said. "And in the act of contrition, you have to be humble, you can't be self-justified. You have to say, 'I'm sorry, ashamed, I know I did wrong and I'll never do it again.'" Clinton bristled at this advice. He said that he felt humbled and stupid for losing, but he saw an obligation to explain and justify all that he had done in the context of the opposition he had faced and the way his actions had been misinterpreted. On one level, he could say, "I screwed up," but on another level, he could rationalize everything that had happened to him. This was bigger than specifics, Morris argued, it was a whole attitude. Clinton relented, agreeing to go ahead with a *mea culpa*, yet he continued to argue with Morris about wording. The suggested language, he complained, was too apologetic.

"Well, you can't say, 'So I robbed the store but I need the money badly because my sister is starving,'" Morris responded. "That's a very nice justification for robbing the store, but it implies that you don't think it was all wrong to rob the store."

"But I don't!" Clinton said.

"But you do!" Morris insisted.

At one point, the two men haggled for several hours over whether the word *apology* should be included in his statement to the voters. He finally delivered the *mea culpa* speech in paid television ads in which he never used direct words of apology, instead turning to a family parable, claiming that when he was growing up, his daddy never had to whup him twice for making the same mistake. He had learned his lesson, he said.

Then he was trying to win back the governorship, now he was struggling to keep his presidency: two situations markedly different in type and magnitude, but it is worth remembering what happened the first time. The reaction to the Arkansas *mea culpa* was swift and sure. Everyone hated it. Clinton's poll ratings dropped more than twenty points within a matter of days. There was pressure on him to withdraw. People said they were disgusted by Clinton after being freshly reminded of his flaws. Morris told Clinton that they should think of the apology as a smallpox vaccination. You'll get sick, but then you're immune. But the consultant did not believe it himself. He thought he had made a fatal mistake and destroyed his client. Then, within several weeks, the anger dissipated, the *mea culpa* was accepted. Clinton was not only forgiven, he was inoculated from future attacks on the very issues that had got him into trouble in the first place.

SEVEN

Good evening. This afternoon in this room, from this chair, I testified before the office of independent counsel and a grand jury. I answered their questions truthfully, including questions about my private life, questions no American citizen would ever want to answer.

Still I must take complete responsibility for all my actions, both public and private. And that is why I am speaking to you tonight.

THE FIRST TWO PARAGRAPHS of the speech sounded prosaic, but they were rich with the subtexts of Clinton's life. Every sentence was in competition with itself over its meaning, a struggle between darkness and light.

The first sentence could be interpreted as an admission of humiliation. Here was Clinton, sitting in a chair in a room that had once served such noble purposes, the Map Room where President Franklin Delano Roosevelt had charted the progress of Allied Forces in Europe, but that now would also be remembered as the room where President Clinton became the first president to testify to a grand jury as the target of a criminal investigation. But for Clinton there was another meaning to those words. The fact that he was sitting in that room, in that chair, was a reminder that he was president, the first two-term Democratic president since

FDR, in fact, and it was an office that he had reached and held on to only through prodigious effort, facing endless challenges against great odds. In that context, testifying before the independent counsel and grand jury was just another challenge for him to endure. What he was seeking to evoke here, despite the unseemly circumstances, was the image of the good soldier and patriot. He viewed his struggle with Kenneth Starr more as a matter of politics than law. Political campaigns tend to imitate the rhetoric of military campaigns, with battles and skirmishes and armies and war rooms, but in Clinton's case the war metaphor runs on a deeper psychological level. The campaign became the equivalent of the war he never fought. It was a means of pardoning his past and making himself feel worthy. This was his toughest battle in the war against Starr.

The second sentence reflected an internal contradiction that is a familiar aspect of Clinton's rhetoric. Leave aside the accuracy of his assertion that he "answered the questions truthfully," including questions about his private life. During his four hours of testimony before Starr and the grand jury, Clinton read a statement acknowledging an inappropriate relationship with Monica Lewinsky, but refused to answer many specific questions about their sexual liaisons near the Oval Office. This sentence in his speech did not say that he answered *all* their questions, but it left that clear implication, especially with the closing phrase about questions that no American citizen would want to answer. Later in the speech, Clinton acknowledged that one of the ways he misled people in the Lewinsky matter was by withholding information—precisely what he was doing again in this sentence.

In the second paragraph, Clinton offered his reason for giving the speech, building his explanation around one of the essential words of his political career—*responsibility*.

From the late 1980s through the years of his presidency, Clinton's political philosophy had been framed by the rhetoric of opportunity and responsibility. They were his effort through semantics to resolve the contradictory impulses of a new Democrat: *opportunity* meaning that he still believed in the basic liberal concept that the government should provide the most opportunities for the greatest number of people; *responsibility* a signal to the vast middle class, which he did not want to alienate, that anyone given an opportunity by the government would be responsible for meeting certain standards. In Arkansas, his model was education: the opportunity was for teachers to get more pay and for students to get more course offerings and smaller class sizes, and the responsibility was for both teachers and students to document their skills through standardized competence tests. He later applied this concept to welfare reform, linking opportunities for work and child care to the responsibility of welfare recipients to take jobs. During his presidential years, he extended the concept into ever-more personal areas, linking the opportunities of expanded education and health-care funding to the responsibility of young adults to turn away from premarital sex and cigarettes.

Clinton's history, however, shows that taking "complete responsibility" for all his actions, "public and private," was not one of his strong points. The examples come from all parts of his life, large and small. In the Lewinsky scandal, the most obvious and disingenuous avoidance of responsibility was in the way that he made one of his aides, Betty Currie, seem more responsible for young Monica's visits to the Oval Office than he was. But lesser examples ran through my mind as I considered that word in his speech. I could not stop thinking about the connection, or disconnection, in Clinton's world between responsibility and time.

Clinton was always late for appointments, meetings, speeches, engagements, dinners, constantly keeping people waiting, without accepting responsibility for what his tardiness meant to others. This habit began during his college days at Georgetown. His friends would plan a dinner or dance and wait for Clinton to show up, and after an hour or two had gone by, he would arrive and casually say that he had been talking to somebody and forgot what time it was, and, usually, his roommate Tom Campbell later recalled, they would discover that he had been "talking to some nincompoop about nothing." His friends stopped expecting Clinton anywhere on time. The habit intensified once he reached elected office, as did his refusal to accept responsibility for the consequences. It was during his first term as Arkansas governor that aides first began talking about "Clinton time"—which was an hour or two behind regular time. They would often lie to him about when he was due somewhere, giving him an earlier time than the actual one, hoping that might keep him on schedule, but it never did. Some appointments were more important not to be late for than others, but Clinton was egalitarian in that regard: he could be as late for a meeting with high-rolling executives as for one with poor farmers.

Once, when Arkansas's powerful poultry barons were upset about a tax proposal, Clinton's staff arranged a summit meeting at the capitol. The hostility that they brought with them to Little Rock only increased once they reached the governor's office and were asked to wait in the lobby until Clinton arrived. He finally got there two hours late. After the tense meeting, Clinton raged at his scheduling staff, blaming them for the disaster. He claimed that the meeting was not on his schedule, until they showed him clearly that it was and that he was at fault. The habit was never broken, but eventually Clinton's aides learned to accept it with gallows humor. One day, the governor's receptionist sent a note to the chief of staff warning him that an uninvited and potentially dangerous visitor was in the capitol building. "Security downstairs holding guy in their office who was sent here to kill the Gov.," her note read. The chief of staff took the note and sent it on to the appointments secretary with a deadpan notation: "See if you can work this guy in."

That is not to say that Clinton is the only politician known for being late. A self-centered sense of time seems to be a prerequisite for the job. But Clinton was more an exaggeration of the political norm. His disregard for time was not just casual, but crossed over a fine line into not taking complete responsibility for his actions. In that regard, as in so many others, his motivation was not wrongheaded or manipulative at first. He was late because he always wanted to talk to one more person, to try to win someone over, to receive more affirmation, to satisfy an immediate desire. The same impulse that made him likable and helped him politically could also make him callous and irresponsible and hurt him in the end. Time and responsibility and Bill Clinton: he said in January that he would answer the Lewinsky questions "sooner rather than later"—and it took him seven months.

EIGHT

As you know, in a deposition in January, I was asked questions about my relationship with Monica Lewinsky. While my answers were legally accurate, I did not volunteer information. Indeed I did have a relationship with Miss Lewinsky that was not appropriate. In fact it was wrong.

THIS PARAGRAPH fairly shouted from Clinton's past. His claim of "legal accuracy" evoked perhaps the most unforgettable, if inconsequential, evasive answer of his political life—his attempt in 1992 to avoid the simple admission that he, like millions of people of his generation, had smoked marijuana. Instead, Clinton insisted at first that he had not broken any state or federal drug laws. It was a technically correct but disingenuous answer, one that he eventually elaborated on by acknowledging that he had "experimented with marijuana a time or two" during his two years in England as a Rhodes scholar, thus not breaking any U.S. laws, though he felt compelled to add that he didn't like it "and didn't inhale."

The next clause in the speech, in which he confessed that he "did not volunteer information," had a deeper resonance, evoking an important aspect of the Clinton enigma. He is an inveterate talker, eager to chat with almost anyone about anything, even willing to tell a national audience about his underwear of choice—

yet throughout his political life he has consistently withheld important information about himself and his office. No sunshine laws for Clinton; he is a one-man darkness unit. In Arkansas, he and Hillary took personal control of every document and scrap of information related to his governorship. Some of the papers were stored at the University of Arkansas–Little Rock for a brief period, but were removed during the 1992 campaign and kept in private storage. One can only shudder at the thought of what historians will have to surmount to win the release of sensitive documents at the future Clinton Presidential Library in Little Rock. Throughout his White House tenure, investigators on Capitol Hill and at the independent counsel's office have been in constant battle with Clinton and his aides over the release of documents and the testimony of key witnesses. When information was forthcoming, often it was released not in the spirit of the public's right to know, but as a political tactic to diminish the impact of disclosures by congressional investigators.

On a more personal level, Clinton's acknowledgment that he "did not volunteer information" brought to mind a sentence in the best-known piece of writing of his career, the December 3, 1969, letter that the then twenty-three-year-old Clinton wrote to Col. Eugene J. Holmes, head of the ROTC program at the University of Arkansas. At the beginning of the letter, Clinton thanked Holmes for saving him from the draft (and a date-certain induction into the Army) by allowing him to enroll in the ROTC program in Fayetteville. The rest of the letter was Clinton's apologetic defense for his subsequent decision to withdraw from the ROTC program and return to Oxford, a maneuver he pulled off when it became obvious to him that he would never be drafted. In one sentence in the letter to Holmes, Clinton wrote, "I began to think I had deceived you, not by lies—there were none—but by failing to tell you all the things I'm writing now." He had failed to tell the colonel that he had left for Oxford with no intentions of ever going back to Fayetteville to serve out his reserve mission, and that he opposed the war and thought the draft was illegitimate, and that he had taken several trips to Washington that summer to plan antiwar demonstrations.

The words in his letter showed he clearly understood that deception could involve more than lies, or legal accuracy. But that did not stop him from continuing the deception. In dealing with the draft issue later in life, as he entered state and national politics, he was plagued more than anything else by what he did not say—omissions in his story. The first act of not volunteering information, or covering it up, came in 1974, his maiden political effort, when he ran for Congress in northwest Arkansas. One of his first tasks was to get back the Holmes letter and any other material in his ROTC file. He thought he had taken care of the potential controversy, not realizing that another officer in the unit had kept a copy of the letter (and would release it eighteen years later). In 1978, when he made his first run for governor, the draft issue was raised by Billy G. Geren, a retired lieutenant colonel in the Air Force, who had served as head of the Arkansas ROTC after Holmes. Geren held a news conference on the capitol steps and denounced Clinton as a draft dodger, but Clinton easily rebuffed the charge by offering a fuzzy response and withholding information. He claimed that he had never received a draft deferment and failed to mention that he had ever been drafted.

Geren was closer to making a strong case than Clinton or the press realized. He had heard about the letter that Clinton had written to Colonel Holmes but could not find a copy of it. Ed Howard, who had been the drill sergeant on the university ROTC staff, recalled that Geren called him at home late one night shortly before the press conference and asked about the Clinton file and the letter. "He wanted me to tell the press that I knew about it," Howard said. But Howard was supporting Clinton in the gubernatorial race and refused Geren's request. The day after the press conference, Howard read in the papers that Clinton denied ever receiving a draft deferment. His reaction was the same as it had been back in 1969 when he first heard about the letter to Holmes. "I was disappointed with Bill," he said. "And angry—again."

Thirteen years later, in the spring of 1991, as Clinton was preparing to run for president, Howard found himself dealing with the issue one more time. He was being pursued by a reporter for the *Arkansas Gazette* who had heard from an ex-student in Fayetteville about the possible existence of a controversial letter from young Bill Clinton concerning the draft. The reporter had called Howard several times, and it was the first thing that crossed Howard's mind when he saw Clinton on Derby Day in Hot Springs that April. Maybe, he thought, he should tell the governor. They shook hands and chatted a minute, and then Howard said that a reporter was on the trail of the letter and the draft.

"Oh, don't worry about that," Clinton said. "I've put that one to bed."

"Okay," said Howard.

There was a pause and then Clinton asked, "What did you tell 'em?"

"Nothing," said Howard.

"Good," Clinton said.

Again in the early days of the 1992 presidential campaign, Clinton did not volunteer the fact that he had been drafted, instead leaving the opposite impression. In an interview with Dan Balz of *The Washington Post*, he said he expected his draft board to send him an induction notice his first year at Oxford "but they never did." When reports emerged that he had indeed been drafted, Clinton alternately said that he had forgotten or did not think it was important, since the induction date had been canceled.

Here, again, Clinton seems an exaggeration of the norm. All human beings have secrets, all have done things that they would prefer were not fully revealed to the world. The public life is built on half-truths, and it is natural for anyone, especially a politician, to try to present himself in the best light. Millions of young American men avoided the draft one way or another, just as millions of people have had extramarital sex. But with Clinton, the tension between reality and image, between what he is and what he wants to be, is so relentless that over the years it became habitual for him to withhold information — justifiably or not.

NINE

It constituted a critical lapse in judgment and a
personal failure on my part for which I am solely
and completely responsible.

THE CORE OF THE CLINTON RIDDLE lies in this sentence, especially in the phrase "a critical lapse in judgment." The wording makes it sound as though his liaison with young Monica Lewinsky was an aberration, a slip from normal behavior, when, in fact, it reflected one of the more familiar traits of his life, a recklessness that seemed to contradict his stated beliefs and imperil his accomplishments.

Clinton, from an early age, believed that he could be president. His second-grade teacher predicted that he would reach the White House. His mother boasted to friends that her boy Billy would run the country someday. His career path seemed set from the morning in August 1963 when he stepped onto the Rose Garden lawn as a delegate to Boys Nation and listened to President Kennedy speak and maneuvered his way into position to shake JFK's hand. At age twenty, he wrote a letter expressing the hope that his achievements would warrant "a little asterisk" by his name "in the billion pages of the book of life." He achieved his goal with amazing speed. At age thirty-two, he became the youngest American governor in the postwar era. At forty-six, he became the third youngest president in American history. When he turned fifty, he was the second-youngest president ever to win a second term.

His rhetoric, from the start, resonated with the themes of right and wrong and the corruptive nature of political power.

In his high school graduation speech, a benediction, Clinton prayed that he and his classmates at Hot Springs High would "keep a high sense of values while wandering through the complex maze which is our society" and "know and care what is right and wrong, so that we can be victorious in this life and rewarded in the next." When he ran for Congress in 1974, while his girl-friend Hillary Rodham worked in Washington for the House Judiciary Committee's inquiry staff preparing the case for President Nixon's impeachment, he declared that Nixon should resign if he lied to the American people. Two years later, running for attorney general in his first successful campaign, he lamented that he had "devoted twelve years to becoming well educated, well disciplined and well motivated in politics" only to arrive on the political scene at a time when "most people believe that politicians are either corruptible, weak or ineffective." The defining theme of his first inaugural address as the young governor of Arkansas was a bold ethical declaration: "For as long as I can remember, I have deplored the arbitrary and abusive exercise of power by those in authority, and I will do what I can to prevent it." At an early age, he understood that sex was one of the ways that powerful men abused their positions. "Politics gives guys so much power and such big egos they tend to behave badly toward women," he told friends at Oxford. "And I hope I never get into that."

All of which leads to one question, asked in various ways. Why? Why would someone who had achieved his lifelong dream needlessly jeopardize it? Why would an inherently cautious politician with an obvious need for public affirmation follow such a careless private path? Why would someone who seemed to have a sophisticated understanding of the roots of public disillusionment, whose rhetoric evoked the struggle against voices of cynicism, fall into patterns of behavior that increased disillusionment and cynicism? Why would someone with a deep distrust of his political enemies give them so much ammunition with which to attack? Why would someone with a near photographic memory, who could immediately recall a telephone number that he had not dialed in thirty years, seem so incapable of remembering and learning from history and his own mistakes?

There are repetitive cycles in Clinton's life and recurring traits in his character that go a long way toward anticipating what he will do and explaining afterward why he did it. The familiar patterns of his personality became apparent starting with his childhood in a troubled family in small-town Arkansas. The traits that first emerged then included his tendency to block things out, to compartmentalize different aspects of his life, to deny reality and create a fantasy life, to keep going no matter what obstacles faced him, and to feel a constant hunger for love and affirmation. Other traits, acquired later, were more common characteristics of many powerful and ambitious men. These include an enormous appetite for life, a sex drive so powerful that some psychologists would classify it as an addiction, a susceptibility to readily available sexual partners attracted to power, a lack of normal standards of self-control, an abuse of the privileges of public office, and a reliance on aides, friends, and family to shield him from the public consequences of his behavior.

These characteristics served contradictory purposes for Clinton. In his perpetual cycle of loss and recovery, the traits that accounted for his success were inseparable from the ones that provoked failure; the drives and impulses coexisted, seemed one and the same. Time and again, in the face of seemingly inevitable disaster, Clinton somehow found the means to recover; there was always a successful ending, he became president, then a two-term president, realizing all his dreams, and his ability to survive only exacerbated a self-delusion of invincibility. It was that characteristic, perhaps above all others, that might have overtaken Clinton during the eighteen months that he had sex near the Oval Office with Monica Lewinsky. "It reminds me of the *Titanic*," said E. James Lieberman, a Washington psychiatrist. "Lots of power. Big. Sexy. Thinks he's invulnerable, like the builders of the ship. And here is this twenty-one-year-old iceberg."

TEN

NATURE OR NURTURE: what does a father mean in the development of character? If he means anything at all, the first clues to the reckless side of Clinton's personality might lie there. During the three years I researched his biography, I struggled with the meaning in his life of William Jefferson Blythe, his biological father. Blythe was a traveling salesman Virginia had met when she had left Hope, Arkansas, to study nursing at Tri-State Hospital in Shreveport. She and Blythe were together for only two months before they got married and he was shipped off to North Africa for service in World War II. Their time together after the war was almost as brief; he was killed in a car accident three months before Bill's birth.

W.J., as Blythe was called, was a generous, freewheeling man about whom Virginia knew almost nothing when she fell for him at first sight, the moment he walked into her hospital. How old was he? He told her he was born February 27, 1918, the date on his gravestone. His military records said he was born on February 21, 1917. What was his background? He told her that he was passing through Shreveport, and that he was so struck by her that he would stay in town, find an apartment, and take a job selling Oldsmobiles. But his military records show that he had been in the Army for two months by the time Virginia first saw him.

Blythe seemed to be constantly reinventing himself, starting over every day, the familiar stranger and ultimate traveling salesman, surviving off charm and affability. Anyone doubting his persuasive powers need know only this: when Virginia brought her parents down to Shreveport to get their blessing for her to marry him, it took him only minutes to win over her skeptical, tough-minded mother, Edith Cassidy. It was a classic wartime wedding, performed in September 1943 by a justice of the peace in Texarkana, bonding two people who knew little about each other's past and less about the future except that they would soon be separated.

Virginia knew that he was a traveling salesman who came off a farm near Sherman, Texas, and that she became "weak-kneed," as she put it, when she saw him—and that is all she knew. She did not know about the December 1935 marriage license filed across the state line in Madill, Oklahoma, recording the marriage of W. J. Blythe and Virginia Adele Gash, a seventeen-year-old daughter of a Sherman tavern owner, or about the divorce papers filed in Dallas a year later, after Adele had left the Sherman farmhouse and W.J. had sent on her clothes in a suitcase. She did not know about the birth certificate filed in Austin, Texas, on January 17, 1938, two years after the divorce, listing W. J. Blythe as the father of Adele Gash's baby boy, Henry Leon Blythe.

Nor did she know about the marriage license filed in Ardmore, Oklahoma, on August 11, 1938, recording the marriage of W. J. Blythe and twenty-year-old Maxine Hamilton, or about Maxine's divorce from Blythe nine months later, in which the judge ruled that W.J. was "guilty of extreme cruelty and gross neglect of duty . . . in that he refused to provide for her a place to live, and within two weeks after their marriage he refused to recognize her as his wife, that he abandoned her and deserted her in Los Angeles, California, and refused to furnish her transportation to her parents in Oklahoma City, Oklahoma." Virginia did not know that in 1940 W.J. married Adele Gash's little sister, Faye, and then divorced her a few months later, though his motivation in that arrangement seemed to be not love but a desire to avoid marrying another young woman who claimed to be pregnant with his baby.

Bill Blythe married Virginia Cassidy without telling her any of that, and within weeks he was gone off to war. In her later recollections, Virginia said that she reunited with Blythe in Shreveport in November 1945 after he had already made a stop in

Sherman after his discharge from the Army. But his military records indicate that he did not arrive home from Italy until December 1 and was honorably discharged at Camp Shelby, Mississippi, on December 7. If he then visited Sherman before his rendezvous with Virginia in Shreveport, it is unlikely, given travel times in those days, that they could have seen each other until December 10. This is inconsequential except for one thing: the timing of the conception of William Jefferson Blythe III—the baby who became Bill Clinton. For years afterward, there were whispers in Hope about who little Billy's father was, rumors spawned by Virginia's flirtatious nature as a young nurse and the inevitable temptation of people to count backward nine months from the birth date to see who was where doing what.

Nine months before August 19, 1946, Army Tech 3 W.J. Blythe was still in Italy. Virginia heard the talk. Her answer was that Billy, who weighed six pounds and eight ounces at birth, was born a month early, induced weeks ahead of schedule because she had taken a fall and the doctor was concerned about her condition.

My curiosity increased after *First in His Class* was published when I began receiving inquiries from the family of a man in Louisiana who said that he had dated a Tri-State nursing graduate in 1945 named Virginia Cassidy from Hope, Arkansas. My reporting on that claim has been inconclusive. I remain an agnostic on the question of Clinton's paternity; the evidence is unclear as to his biological father: Blythe, the Louisiana man, or someone else. Other events, especially Bill's decision to change his name from Blythe to Clinton at age fifteen, during a period when his mother was divorced from Roger Clinton and Bill was urging her not to reconcile with him, led me to suspect that he shared my curiosity about his biological father. It was one of many questions I wanted to talk to him about if he ever gave me another interview.

In any case, Bill Clinton essentially grew up without a father. His mother married Roger Clinton when Bill was four, but Roger did not legally adopt him and rarely spent time with him. Roger, who briefly ran a car dealership in Hope and supplied Virginia's father's store with bootleg whiskey, was a sharpie from Hot Springs who lived up to his nickname "Dude." He was a natty dresser, his face splashed with cologne, who loved to drink and gamble and have a good time. Much like Bill Blythe, he had a previous life that Virginia either did not know about or repressed. When they began dating, he was still married and had two step-sons. When his first wife, Ina Mae Murphy, filed for divorce, she charged in court papers that Roger had abused her, once smashing her in the face with her high-heeled shoes, leaving her with a black eye and a bloody scalp. Virginia did discover before she married Roger that he was a philanderer and once burst into an apartment after being tipped off by a friend that he had been entertaining a stewardess there. She found the room empty but strewn with provocative lingerie, which she took outside and angrily hung on the clothesline to embarrass the woman.

Still, she decided to marry him, much to her family's dismay. "I'm fixin' to marry Roger Clinton," she told her favorite uncle, Buddy Grisham, who later remembered the rest of the conversation this way: "I told her, 'No,' I said, 'you're not fixin' to do that.' Roger was in the Buick business, so I said, 'You're fixin' to marry a bunch of Buick cars!' She could have a new car to drive whenever she wanted—these women give in to that . . . I told her she'd have hell from then on." That was mild compared with her mother Edith's reaction. She threatened to seek custody of Billy and even consulted a lawyer about how she could do it. The custody threat never made it to court, but it did sever the family. When Virginia Blythe became Virginia Clinton on June 19, 1950, her parents and son Billy were not at the ceremony.

Billy called Roger "Daddy," but Roger was gone a lot, and when he was home, he often sat alone in a room or argued with Virginia. One night, Virginia dressed Billy up to take him to the hospital to visit her grandmother, who was dying. Roger did not want them to leave. When Virginia said she was going anyway, he hauled out a gun and fired a shot over her head into the wall. Virginia went across the street and called the police. Billy slept at a neighbor's house. Roger spent the night in jail. Soon thereafter, having run his car business into the red, Roger moved his family back to Hot Springs, where he supervised the parts department in his brother Roy's larger Buick dealership. His drinking worsened year by year, until the family reached a critical point of crisis when Bill was fifteen.

In April 1962, Virginia fled from Roger, taking Bill and his younger brother, Roger Clinton, Jr., to a new house that she had bought with money she had saved furtively, expecting this day would come. In seeking to end the marriage on grounds of mental cruelty and abuse, she testified that Roger's drinking had led to two violent eruptions, first at a dance when he became drunk and kicked her and struck her, then at home when he "threw me to the floor and began to stomp me, pulled my shoe off and hit me on the head several times." She left him for a day after that incident, she said, but took him back when he "promised to quit drinking and treat me with love." Bill not only comforted his mother during these troubles, he offered her strong testimonial support for the divorce. In his own affidavit, he stated that he was familiar with his stepfather's habitual drinking and had witnessed the second assault on his mother. "I was present . . . and it was I who called my mother's attorney who in turn had to get the police to come to the house to arrest the defendant," he said in a deposition.

Roger broke his earlier promise to quit drinking, and Bill testified that he was called in for help again at a Christmas party at the house of a family friend. Virginia said Roger humiliated her that night with verbal abuse. "I was finally able to get my oldest son Billy to help me with the car and finally able to take him home," she said. Roger's explosions were most often jealous rages. Although a notorious womanizer himself, he constantly accused his wife of being unfaithful. Virginia was a naturally affectionate woman who loved to hug and schmooze and flirt. As a nurse anesthetist on call whenever the doctors needed her for surgery, she kept odd hours that made Roger suspicious. His distrust was exacerbated by reports he would get from friends that they had seen Virginia drinking coffee with this doctor or that medical supplies dealer.

Billy came to understand that if the violence and abuse were to end, he had to be the one to stop them. He was an adolescent put in the position of reversing roles so that, as he later said, "I was the father." Decades later, Clinton and his mother would recount what they described as a pivotal confrontation between Billy and Roger when Billy was fourteen. According to that later story, Billy stormed into his parents' bedroom one evening when he heard his stepfather yelling at his mother, demanded that Roger stand and face him, and ordered Roger never to strike his mother again. Virginia claimed afterward that this confrontation put an end to the physical abuse, though the divorce transcripts indicate that

Roger continued to torment and threaten her and Billy in the following months. In Bill's affidavit, taken a few weeks before the divorce but several months after the night when he dressed down his stepfather, he recounted more fights.

"On one occasion last month I again had to call my mother's attorney because of the defendant's conduct causing physical abuse to my mother and the police again had to be summoned to the house," he stated. "He has threatened my mother on a number of occasions and because of his nagging, arguing with my mother I can tell that she is very unhappy and it is impossible in my opinion for them to continue to live together as husband and wife. The last occasion in which I went to my mother's aid when he was abusing my mother he threatened to mash my face in if I took her part."

Two months after Virginia won a divorce from Roger, she took him back. He was ensconced in the house on Scully Street, and everyone there legally carried his name, even Bill, the boy he had never adopted. But it was not his castle. He lived there more now as a tolerated guest, a boarder. By the time Bill began his senior high school year in the fall of 1963, everything in the house revolved around the golden son. Roger Clinton would sit for hours at night in a swivel chair in the rec room on the far side of the dinette in the back of the house, a tumbler of liquor at his side, watching television through trifocal glasses or listening to his collection of jazz records. In his younger days, when he was cool and handsome, he had spent most of his after-hours partying at downtown clubs. Now his drinking was more private. He stashed liquor miniatures around the house and in tool bins at the auto parts shop.

In the literature on children of alcoholics, there is a type sometimes referred to as the Family Hero, who plays one of two well-defined roles, either as caretaker and protector of the family or as its redeemer to the outside world. As protector, the Family Hero, usually the oldest child, assumes adult responsibilities and provides an anchor of coherence to siblings and parents, leading to an attitude that things are always better, the family safer, when this person is in charge. As redeemer, the Family Hero is often excused from the family's inner burdens and dispatched into the world to excel and to return with praise and rewards that will make the entire unit feel worthy. In this role, the Family Hero be-

comes a vessel of ambition and the repository of hope. Bill Clinton, during his high school years, was the prototype of the Family
Hero in both definitions.

Many of the traits he took into his adult life and political career, for better and worse, make more sense when seen from this
perspective. Along with his burning ambition for public life came
a sense that things were better when he was in control. This righ-
teousness, born from his relationship with an alcoholic stepfather,
also served as a way for Clinton to ignore his own failings. Decades
later, when he shaped his *mea culpa* in Arkansas around the line
that his daddy never had to whup him twice for making the same
mistake, he was evoking a family relationship that never existed.
Roger Clinton, the daddy to whom he was referring, whupped
Bill now and again, but the whippings came in moments of
drunken rage, not as a means of correcting the young man's behavior.

The effect was the opposite of what fatherly discipline is intended to have: Clinton began developing a sense that he was always right and that any accusations against him or attempts to
punish him were misguided. It became second nature for him to
assert his innocence and place blame on others, even in the
smallest incidents. In touch football games, he was always claiming that he had touched the runner or, if he was carrying the ball,
that the defender had missed him. If he was walking down the
street with a pal and they went through a rain puddle and water
sprayed on Clinton's pants, his first reaction was to say that his
friend splashed him on purpose. If the girl next door, in getting
out of Clinton's car, accidentally knocked his new saxophone
case onto the ground and dented it, his instinctive response again
was to say that she had done it on purpose.

It was also in dealing with the trauma of Roger's alcoholism
that Clinton developed another trait that he carried with him into
his adult career: the ability to block out problems and deny reality
as a means of keeping going. He never talked about his father outside the home; his high school friends came over to the Clinton
house every week for years without knowing that anything was
amiss.

ELEVEN

THE DUALITY OF LIFE FOR CLINTON was also mirrored in the two women who raised him in his infancy and the town where he later grew up. His first four formative years in Hope were shaped by two strong women who fought for his attention and represented the competing forces that would shape his life. His mother, the young widow Virginia, was irrepressible and fun-loving, determined not to let her predicament as a single mother slow her down. His grandmother, Edith Cassidy, who took care of him for long stretches while his mother studied advanced nursing in New Orleans, a city she loved, was temperamental and frustrated by her position in life. Virginia carried and bore baby Billy, but once he was brought home to the Cassidy house on Hervey Street in Hope, Edith assumed that she was in control. Virginia might escape to walk him in the stroller or rock with him on the front porch, but when he was in the house, Edith ordered his life. She had him eating and drinking at assigned times, pushing food in his mouth if necessary, and his sleep was regulated to the minute, napping and waking with metronomic discipline. He took attributes from both women—the freewheeling spirit of his mother, the stubborn will of his grandmother—with him into adult life.

Another aspect of duality and contradiction was evident in the city where he spent most of his youth, Hot Springs, a cosmopolitan resort town that was unlike anywhere else in Arkansas, a city of secrets and vapors and bathhouses and deep forests and

ancient corruption and opportunity. Hope, the town where Clinton was born, represented the idealistic side of his nature. During
the summers of his adolescence, as relief from the tension in his
family, he got on the Trailways bus and rode back down to Hope.
James Morgan, an Arkansan who ghostwrote Virginia's autobiog-
raphy, Leading with My Heart, once told me that when he interviewed President Clinton for that book, one of Clinton's strongest
childhood memories was riding south from Hot Springs to Hope,
and that the joy he felt during those trips explained why he copied
them during his 1992 campaign by taking bus trips across the
American heartland.

But Hope is largely a myth in the Clinton story. Hot Springs
explains the Clinton enigma. Virtue and sin coexisted there; the
largest illegal gambling operation in the South operated side by
side with dozens of Baptist churches, some of them funded with
gambling money. Hot Springs is a place where once, when I
asked the town historian, Inez Cline, for information on someone, the spunky grandmother headed off to a file cabinet and said,
"Let's see, why don't we look under 'Gangsters.'" It is a place where
Dick Hildreth, a leather-faced masseur at the Arlington Hotel
bathhouse, once described to me his intention to vote for Clinton
in the idiom of an old gambler who once gave rubdowns to Lucky
Luciano, Meyer Lansky, and the Capone boys from Chicago.
"Yeah," he said, "I think I'll make a play on Billy this year." It is
where a former mayor, Melinda Baran, a contemporary of Clinton's, once told me that "every family in town has a skeleton rat-
tling around in the closet," and then went on to describe how her
grandfather had been a member of the political machine that
made the city safe for gamblers and mobsters.

It is a place that inspired a poetic memoir titled The Book-
maker's Daughter, by Shirley Abbott, who was exactly that—the
daughter of a bookie who would leave for the office every morning saying with only the slightest hint of irony that he was off to
make an honest buck. Hot Springs, Abbott wrote, "deconstructs
and demolishes the American dream of virtue and hard work
crowned by success, as well as all platitudes and cant about
the democratic process and small-town American life. After
an upbringing here, New York city politics, or Watergate, or
even the savings and loan scandal, could hardly come as a
surprise." She wrote those words long before Whitewater or Mon-

ica Lewinsky became part of Clinton's story and the American lexicon.

By the time the first Clinton arrived from the small Arkansas town of Dardanelle in 1919, sin had been flourishing in Hot Springs for a half-century. Central Avenue was lined with ornate bathhouses on one side and betting parlors on the other. Gambling was illegal but open, as was prostitution. Both enterprises funded the local government. On the twenty-seventh of each month, officers would round up prostitutes and march them over to the courthouse, where, in the words of an old judge, "every young blade in town was there to look them over." The prostitutes would pay five bucks, their madams twenty, and then go back to business. The gambling entrepreneurs made their payoffs in quieter fashion. It was said they had to bribe a string of thirteen judges, cops, and public officials.

There were four Clinton brothers in town between the two world wars, including Roger, who would later become Bill's stepfather, and Raymond, who rose to the highest prominence as a civic leader and Buick dealer. Raymond was a sharp-eyed financier who at times challenged the status quo but knew how to accommodate the powers that be when that better suited his purposes. He had been well aware of the gangland presence in Hot Springs since the days when he worked as a downtown sales clerk as a young man. "I was working in a drugstore back in the early twenties when Al Capone used to come down, walk down the street with his hat . . . turning his hat down . . . and he would have two men behind him and two in front and two on each side," Raymond Clinton recalled in a 1980 interview.

Capone and other notorious mobsters made frequent visits to the spa in provincial Arkansas. They felt protected in the valley of hot waters. Federal agents and Chicago detectives would tail them down to Hot Springs, but for the most part there was an uneasy truce once they reached town. It was a common sight at the bathhouses for cops and criminals to be resting side by side on massage tables, getting rubdowns, chatting amiably. Raymond Clinton appreciated one aspect of the gangland presence after he opened his Buick dealership. "I did a lot of business with them," he said. "They bought a lot of cars."

Stories of the decline of men like Roger Clinton, drawn inescapably to the gambling and drinking and nightlife, were familiar tales in Hot Springs. His two pals were Van Hampton Lyell, who operated the Coca-Cola plant, and Gabe Crawford, who ran a drugstore chain. Both had more money than Roger, but shared his traits. For a time, Crawford was married to Roger's niece. When he was drunk, he would beat her. Drinking and wife abuse seemed to be part of the culture of Hot Springs during the fifties and early sixties, according to Judy Ellsworth, whose husband later became mayor. The city, Ellsworth said, was "full of a lot of angry, repressed women" who had been mistreated by their husbands. The men "got away with anything they wanted to. They had no respect for women. They all had mistresses. They all beat their wives. It was the tradition of this city. The men had a way of compartmentalizing their lives. Honesty was never a trait with them. It was never-never land."

Virginia was by no means immune to those troubles. She struggled with her roustabout husband and with some doctors who did not like dealing with a female professional. But she had a duality in her own nature that made her an interesting combination of the contradictory forces of her town. She was devoted to learning and self-improvement, and from an early age pushed her son Bill to excel, often boasting that he would be president someday. But she had an exotic side to her as well, driving around town in Buick convertibles, dyeing her hair with a bright white streak, building a sunken bathtub in her house, sunning herself outside in a tank top. She found the flashy side of Hot Springs irresistible: she enjoyed the shows at the Vapors, liked to drink and gamble at the Belvedere Country Club, and became a regular at the Oaklawn racetrack, where she placed two-dollar bets.

For every shadow of darkness in Hot Springs, there was a corresponding ray of light. The same springs that drew the gamblers to town also brought a rich mix of tourists and new residents from all over the country and Europe, giving the city a cosmopolitan flair that excited young Bill Clinton to the possibilities of the outside world. The sophisticated nature of the town attracted an excellent corps of teachers to Hot Springs High, one of the elite public schools in the state. While many schools in Arkansas were so backward they offered no foreign languages and gave students credit for parking cars at football games, Hot Springs High offered Latin, which Clinton studied for four years, all the higher mathematics courses, and sophisticated world events classes in which

Clinton and his classmates examined the early stages of the Vietnam War.

The status of Bill Clinton within his nuclear family during his high school days was in that sense not unusual. It reflected the middle-American cultural inclinations of the time, when towns gilded their teenagers with the status of golden youth, destined to better futures than the generation before, demigods of the classroom and playing field, their daily lives primed for competition and rewards. The dark and sleazy nights of adult Hot Springs were countered by the icons of innocent youth, of Cook's ice cream parlor and the A&W Drive-In along Albert Pike, of the forest lookout and parking hideaways on the mountain ridge above downtown, of the pep rallies, concerts, dances, and festivals at the Gothic red brick high school. The feel of the town and the generational aspirations of middle-class parents convinced Clinton and his classmates that they owned the world. They were the Chosen Ones—made to feel different and better.

The characteristics that Clinton carried with him into his adult life from his experiences in Hot Springs had both positive and negative effects over the years. His capacity to block out and compartmentalize his life—and to develop a personality in which he could accommodate contradictory thoughts and modes of behavior—helps explain his optimism in the face of difficulties and his remarkable ability to recover from setbacks. But it also gave him the propensity to drift into his own version of never-never land: trying to avoid and deny unpleasant facts, ignoring necessary but unwanted personal advice from friends and advisers, and at times acting as though they and the problem they wanted to discuss with him did not exist. Many people close to Clinton would describe a similar trivial scene to illustrate that larger tendency: Clinton would be seated at a table, eating voraciously, and would neither look at them nor acknowledge what they were saying to him. Betsey Wright, his longtime aide in Arkansas, said she once became so frustrated by this peculiar little habit of denial—he was loudly champing on ice cubes while ignoring her—that she slapped a chunk of ice out of his hand.

TWELVE

ONE OF THE OBVIOUS EXAMPLES of Clinton's tendency toward denial, with more important consequences, came during the previously mentioned 1987 episode when he was on the verge of announcing for president until Betsey Wright confronted him with a list of women who might create the same sort of public embarrassment that drove Gary Hart out of the race. Only when he was confronted directly with a twice-vetted list of problematic women, and was at last unable to block out the problem, did Clinton back away from the presidential starting line that year, explaining to his supporters and the press that he did not think he and his family were quite ready for national exposure. Until being dissuaded at the last moment, Clinton believed that he could get away with something that Hart could not. His extramarital sex life had been an issue bubbling near the surface in every campaign he had ever run. Even in his first race for Congress in 1974, one year before he and Hillary Rodham were married, Clinton would be ushering one of his Arkansas girlfriends out the side door of his campaign headquarters while Rodham was walking in the front, according to the accounts of several people who worked in that campaign. But from the start he had never really had to face the consequences of his behavior.

This only intensified his self-delusionary sense of invincibility, a familiar trait among successful politicians, according to several presidential scholars. Political scientist Charles O. Jones of the University of Wisconsin said he believed that Clinton came to think of himself as beyond penalty for his sexual behavior, and from this came the hubris that led to Monica Lewinsky. "It seems that he ran along the edge of what most of us would judge to be proper for many years there and never really had to suffer politically for it," Jones told me. Historian Robert Dallek, whose second volume of a biography of Lyndon Baines Johnson, *Flawed Giant*, came out a month after the Lewinsky story broke, said that in that regard Clinton reminded him of Johnson. "I think what operates with both these men is that they've gotten so far without being brought down by whatever their transgressions are that there is a built-in assumption that they will keep going and go on forever. Sure there are allegations, but these guys go on and on, so why change?" While not relating his thoughts directly to Clinton or the issue of sex, presidential scholar Michael Beschloss noted that political leaders, "unlike most mortals, are surrounded by people who affirm them all day long, and this can cause a leader to feel invulnerable in ways that other human beings don't."

THE EVIDENCE that Clinton, with all his intelligence and political savvy, could not control a behavior pattern that clearly endangered him has led some experts to conclude that he might have a sexual addiction. The American Psychiatric Association has declined to categorize sexual addiction as a medical diagnosis, citing a lack of sufficient evidence. Even defining the problem is difficult. Some psychiatrists dismiss the term as phony or misleading. How is it to be defined? A celibate priest who is overtaken by the sexual urge once every three months might seek treatment for obsession, while a man having sex three times a day might consider himself normal.

In any case, there are many people who suffer from an inability to control their sexual drive. Brian Doyle, clinical professor of psychiatry at Georgetown University Medical School, told me that he sees patients "in whom lust overcomes their better judgment—some people for whom that happens regularly, no matter what is at stake. Sometimes the results are comical and sometimes they are tragic." Doyle said some experts now think of repetitive compulsive sexual behavior as an impulse control problem in the same spectrum of disorders as obsessive-compulsive behavior.

People suffering from obsessive-compulsive disorders can compartmentalize their lives in the extreme; they might spend hours washing their hands in the bathroom while the kitchen sink remains a mess for weeks. That might serve as a metaphor for Clinton: so cautious in some aspects of his life and so sloppy in others.

During at least one period of his life, there is some evidence that Clinton actively examined his own behavior. He was the governor of Arkansas then, in 1984, and his brother Roger had been convicted and imprisoned on drug charges and was being treated for cocaine addiction. Roger had been arrested during a carefully planned sting operation by the state police, which Clinton had known about ahead of time. He did not warn Roger, nor did he try to stifle the probe, believing that his brother had to deal with the consequences of his own actions.

As part of Roger's treatment, Bill and their mother, Virginia, joined in the counseling sessions. For the first time, the mother and her two sons talked openly about addiction and the effects it had had on the family. Roger was not the first addicted personality in the family. Virginia's mother, Edith, had been addicted to morphine during the final years of her life. During those counseling sessions it came out that Virginia had developed a tendency to avoid unpleasant truths and block out difficult parts of her life, and Bill realized that he had the same characteristics, including the denial mechanism. "We learned a lot about how you do a lot of damage to yourself if you're living with an alcoholic and you just sort of deny that behavior and deflect it all," he told me during a 1992 interview. "You pay a big price for that."

Clinton delved into the literature of addiction and codependence, the emerging fashionable theory, which placed addiction in the realm of family relationships. He often came back to the governor's office talking about the latest book he had read and relating it to his own experience. It was the first time his aides had heard him talking about alcoholism in his home and how it had made him so averse to conflict, why he was always trying to please people. "He was fascinated by it," Betsey Wright told me. "It rang so true that it was kind of like he was being introduced to something that he wished he had known a long time ago." This did not mean that Clinton changed his behavior, Wright said, but simply that he "could see what he was doing far better."

It was in a discussion during that period with his longtime

friend Carolyn Yeldell Staley that Clinton came close to acknowledging the possibility that he had an addiction. "I think we're all addicted to something," Clinton told her. "Some people are addicted to drugs. Some to power. Some to food. Some to sex. We're all addicted to something."

The strongest case that Clinton has a sexual addiction was made by Jerome D. Levin, an expert on rehabilitation counseling who teaches at the New School for Social Research in New York and serves as director of the Alcoholism and Substance Abuse Counselor Training Program. In his recent book, *The Clinton Syndrome*, Levin argues that "Clinton's background as a child of addiction predisposed him biologically and socially to an addiction of his own," that his "sexual proclivities over a lifetime were expansive and developed the strength and persistence of habit," and that specific stresses in his life before and after he began his relationship with Monica Lewinsky—stresses that included the deaths of his mother, Virginia, his friend and political ally Ron Brown, and Israeli prime minister Yitzhak Rabin—made him "highly vulnerable to acting out once again his sexually addictive behavior."

Sexual addictions, Levin argues, are in essence not about sex, but about traits that are to varying degrees evident in Clinton. "They are about insecurity, low self-esteem, and the need for affirmation and reassurance. The sex addict feels unloved and unlovable and therefore looks obsessively for proof that this is not so." The sex addict, according to Levin, "disguises feelings of worthlessness from himself and from the world" and uses sex "to deaden and avoid psychological pain and conflict, reassure and bolster fragile self-esteem, and bury deeply embedded feelings of self-hatred."

Whether sex can be an addiction or not, there is ample evidence of powerful men whose political ambitions seemed matched only by their sexual appetites. One need look no further than Kennedy and Johnson to find examples among Clinton's predecessors in the White House. Viewed in the context of these two, Clinton could argue that he faced an unfair burden. The culture of the times allowed John F. Kennedy and Johnson to avoid even a minute's worth of public controversy over their sexual behavior. JFK's extramarital affairs have been documented and recounted so often in the decades since his death that they are now treated as

just another part of American lore, as familiar as his inaugural address and assassination. Johnson, according to historian Robert
Dallek, was determined not to be outdone by Kennedy. When
LBJ was majority leader of the Senate, he maintained what he
called his "nooky room" in the Capitol for his illicit liaisons. And
when people told him tales of Kennedy's womanizing, Johnson
would pound the table and exclaim, "Goddamn it, I had more
women by accident than he ever had by design!"

For political leaders with strong sexual drives, the availability
of willing partners always seems to be there, whether by accident
or design. From the moment Clinton became governor of Arkansas
in 1979, he was constantly surrounded by eager women. Rudy
Moore, his first chief of staff, said the governor's office was visited
regularly by an array of provocative women, "hangers-on who
could get you in trouble." Randy White, Clinton's first travel aide,
said the governor enjoyed nothing more than to go out on the
road, where he could frequent clubs late at night, his table encircled
by women drawn to the powerful young leader of Arkansas. "He
loved the road," White said.

From those early days through the Lewinsky scandal, some
of Clinton's aides and advisers, including his wife, found themselves working at contradictory purposes. Within his private orbit,
they tried to shield him from his own most reckless instincts, re-
moving sexual temptation whenever possible. This was evident
during his days as governor, when Hillary Clinton and Betsey
Wright attempted to circumscribe his daily actions. A male friend
of Clinton's noticed that Hillary classified the people around Bill
as either "one of the goods or one of the bads. If you were bad, you
had to be kept away from Bill, because if he was with the bad guys,
he would relax and enjoy himself and make comments about at-
tractive women waving at him in the crowd."

Wright took on the role of the bossy big sister. She was constantly checking on his whereabouts, sending out scouts to see
what he was doing and what his enemies were saying about him.
When he was on the road, she would often call his room late at
night to see if he was there. Clinton chafed at her efforts to control his actions. When she insisted that he not go out on jogs
alone, where he might disappear from sight for a few hours, Clinton shouted, "I won't have it! I won't have it!" The effort to protect
Clinton from Clinton continued in his White House years. The

reason that Monica Lewinsky was transferred out of the White House and over to the Pentagon was that Evelyn Lieberman, a Clinton aide who served the first lady's interests on the staff, became concerned about the young woman's flirtatious nature and the president's response to her.

Yet whenever sexual allegations about Clinton reached a crisis point, the women around Clinton, Hillary Clinton and Betsey Wright in particular, served as his chief defenders, dismissing the stories, attacking the accusers, drafting responses, rallying the troops to his cause. Wright spent all of 1992 as a one-person damage control operation, ferreting out potential problems on the Clinton sex front, looking for what she called, with typical sarcasm, "bimbo eruptions." Hillary's role as defender and perhaps enabler, which will be examined in detail later, was more pivotal. Presidential scholar Jones calls all of this "the protective patina" — a phenomenon that surrounds all political leaders to varying degrees and that was particularly apparent in Clinton's career. His wife and other aides worked tirelessly to get him and themselves to the heights they eventually achieved in the White House, running the country, and to get there they had to come to Clinton's defense again and again, one of the patterns of his career.

THIRTEEN

*But I told the grand jury today, and I say to you
now, that at no time did I ask anyone to lie, to hide
or destroy evidence, or to take any other unlawful
action.*

WHAT I THOUGHT of when Clinton came to that line in his speech
was the infamous declaration of innocence that Richard Nixon
uttered during the Watergate scandal: *I am not a crook.* One of the
main reasons I wanted to write a biography of Clinton was to use
his life, and Hillary's, as a means of exploring the rites of passage
of the postwar baby boom generation: following them through the
mythical quiescence of the fifties, the moral awakening of civil
rights, the fervor of Kennedy's New Frontier, the Vietnam quag-
mire, and the depths of Watergate on into confusing adulthood.
For many baby boomers who emerged from those trying times,
Watergate stood as a mountain of shared memory, visible forever
and from every angle as the symbol of arrogance and the abuse of
power.

And now here was Bill Clinton, the ultimate baby boomer,
the first in his generational class to reach the presidency, issuing a
hauntingly Nixonian line from inside the White House. It was
one of the phrases in the speech that prompted David Broder, my
colleague at *The Washington Post*, who covered Nixon and Clinton, to write an excoriating column under the headline TRULY

NIXONIAN. Broder's voice has always been one of moderation, but Clinton's speech sent him into a rhetorical rage in which he said that in one way Clinton was even worse than Nixon. "Nixon's actions, however neurotic and criminal, were motivated by and connected to the exercise of presidential power. He knew the place he occupied, and he was determined not to give it up to those he regarded as his 'enemies,'" Broder wrote. "Clinton acted—and still, even in his supposed mea culpa, acts—as if he does not recognize what it means to be president of the United States. This office he sought all his life, for what? To hit on an intern about the age of his own daughter . . . ?"

Clinton's transgressions do not approach the importance of Watergate. Even if the worst were to be proven—that he not only had sex with Monica Lewinsky and lied about it, as he has now confessed to, but also encouraged others to lie as well, and obstructed justice in trying to cover it up, and in so doing was following a long-standing pattern of concealment and cover-up in matters related to his sex life and Whitewater—that worst-case scenario, entirely possible, still would not place his scandal in the realm of Nixon's. I agree with my colleagues Bob Woodward and Carl Bernstein, who together broke many of the Watergate stories, when they assert that the two cases are not comparable. Watergate was an attempt to subvert the Constitution and the workings of democracy, in which secret police operations were conceived in the White House, political opponents were harassed by agents of the government, the FBI and CIA were involved in covering up officially sanctioned crimes, burglaries were committed, and hush money was paid to agents to silence them.

Yet the very fact that moral comparisons are being made between Nixon and Clinton reveals the vast distance between the idealism that Clinton and Hillary Rodham shared in 1974 and the situation they find themselves in now. Before Clinton took office, he promised that his would be the most ethical administration in history. Whitewater, Lewinsky, two cabinet secretaries indicted, three more under investigation by special prosecutors, his handpicked second-in-command at the Justice Department convicted and imprisoned, investigators still looking into the questionable fund-raising techniques used by Clinton and Vice President Al Gore during the 1996 reelection campaign—it would be hard for anyone to argue that the promise was fulfilled. This ethical failure starved the hope of many of Clinton's generational peers, who thought somehow that their turn in power might be different, while at the same time it fed the vengeful appetites of his ideological adversaries, who had been hungering for this moment since Nixon's fall.

Clinton and Rodham were not distant observers in the events of the Watergate era, they were active participants; Watergate was a seminal event in the shaping of their careers in public life. It was in 1974, during the heat of Watergate, that Clinton made his first run for public office, campaigning for Congress in northwest Arkansas's third congressional district, which then included Hot Springs and Fayetteville, where he was teaching at the law school. During the Democratic primary and in the fall campaign against John Paul Hammerschmidt, the Republican incumbent, Clinton pounded away on the themes of ethics and morality.

"If people demand a more honest politics, they'll get it," he declared at his announcement speech in Hot Springs. Later that spring, he delivered a speech called "Morality in Politics" to a meeting of the Arkansas Council for Social Studies. "Too many people in the Nixon administration believed that morality has no place in politics," he said. "It wasn't that they didn't know the difference between right and wrong—they didn't care. They placed efficiency and effectiveness above honesty and ethics. It is up to the Congress and the American people to preserve other values by restraining the exercise of power by large government . . . otherwise, democracy cannot be preserved." By midsummer, he was saying Nixon should resign if he lied to the American people. After Nixon had resigned and Ford had pardoned him, Clinton called the pardon "an unfortunate and totally unwarranted interruption of the due process of law."

The pardon "set an unwise precedent for the future," Clinton said, "and it may have an unforeseen and damaging impact on pending trials of Watergate defendants. It will have a devastating impact on the families of those who acted for Mr. Nixon and with his knowledge and consent, who are now in jail or are about to go to jail. It will weaken the people's faith in the fair operation of our legal system. While I have not been anxious for Mr. Nixon himself to be in prison, I strongly feel Mr. Jaworski [the special Watergate prosecutor] and the grand jury should have been left free to do their duty and Mr. Nixon forced to respond to any charges that might have been raised against him before President Ford intervened to prevent any jail term."

Once during that election a reporter for the *Arkansas Gazette* followed Bill Clinton on a swing through the Ozarks and watched him campaign among the people of the hill country. They reached an old man sitting near a woodburning stove, who scowled when he realized that the young fellow trying to shake his hand was a politician. "If you're as crooked as the rest of them, I don't want a damn thing to do with you," the old man said. "I'm not old enough yet to be crooked," Clinton responded, an answer that at once was lighthearted and reflected the sensibilities of a generation that thought it was ennobled by its very youth.

While Clinton had been roaming the back highways of northwest Arkansas that spring and summer in search of votes, Hillary Rodham was holed up in an office on Capitol Hill in Washington, surrounded by documents, protected by a double line of security, her movements circumscribed by the sensitivity of her mission as one of thirty-nine lawyers constructing a case for the removal of President Nixon. More than twelve hours a day and seven days a week, Rodham worked at a desk in a mildewed suite on the second floor of the old Congressional Hotel. She rarely associated with anyone outside the closed circle of legal compatriots brought to Washington by John Doar, special counsel for the House Judiciary Committee's impeachment inquiry staff.

Rodham was only twenty-six, less than a year out of Yale Law School, untested in the legal community, yet playing a coveted if minor role in the century's most gripping presidential drama. She did not arrive at the inquiry staff a complete stranger. She and Doar had met the previous spring, when Rodham and Clinton had served on the board of directors of the Barristers Union at Yale Law and invited Doar to judge that year's student Prize Trial. She and Clinton had both been recruited to join the inquiry staff, but Clinton had declined, more eager to begin his own political career in Arkansas; he had even expressed some concern to friends about whether it would hurt him to have a girlfriend working for Nixon's impeachment.

Doar organized the staff into two sections at first. Most of the lawyers were assigned to task forces in the section called Factual Investigation, which was to collect and examine evidence on activities that fell under the rubric of Watergate, including the break-in itself, the alleged cover-up, the use of other dirty tricks in the 1972 campaign, as well as several non-Watergate concerns, including the secret bombing of Cambodia. Rodham was placed in a smaller section known as Constitutional and Legal Research. Its first major project was to research the constitutional grounds for impeachment, an important but scholarly task that not everyone was eager to do.

Rodham's section analyzed the constitutional intent of impeachment and its historical basis in four hundred years of English history. Virtually every word in their report delineating the grounds for impeachment carried weight. At one meeting, they spent four hours arguing over whether to use the phrase "to the modern ear" in describing how high crimes and misdemeanors should be interpreted. Their report concluded that "to limit impeachable conduct to criminal offenses would be incompatible with the evidence concerning the constitutional meaning of the phrase . . . and would frustrate the purpose that the framers intended for impeachment." They found that in thirteen American impeachment cases, including ten of federal judges, fewer than one-third of the articles of impeachment explicitly charged the violation of a criminal statute.

The thoroughness of the report impressed Doar, who believed that the precise wording of articles of impeachment would be of supreme importance. Rodham became one of his staff favorites. It did not matter that she had a partisan past, that she had worked for George McGovern in 1972, for she seemed discreet in her demeanor, reverent of the process, and impartial about the outcome of the endeavor, at least in front of the boss. Doar was a nonpartisan appointment: a moderate Republican who had held a high-profile role in the Justice Department's civil rights division during the 1960s, and from his staff he demanded objectivity and discretion. Just report the facts. He pounded into his staff the notion that they had to show respect for the office of the president. Even in private conversations, they were to refer to Nixon only as the president.

The methodical approach that Doar took was in itself a point of tension. He was so intent on avoiding the appearance of being out to get Nixon that some Democrats on the Judiciary Committee referred to him sarcastically as "the Republican counsel." They preferred the style of one of his three senior associate special counsels, Richard Cates, a trial attorney and professor from Madison, Wisconsin, who had been brought in to help Chairman Peter Rodino decide whether and how to proceed with the inquiry before Doar arrived. Cates was willing to draw conclusions about the evidence that had already been accumulated from the Senate Watergate Committee hearings and earlier investigative work. Doar started with a blank slate. Cates was a master of the story line. He spent hours each day developing theories, placing details in their probable context. Doar, in the words of Rodham's office mate, Tom Bell, "didn't give a whit about" the story. He was looking for detail after detail, assuming that when he was done, the story would take care of itself.

Both styles rubbed off on Rodham. Among the inquiry staff of ninety lawyers, researchers, and clerks, she seemed the least perturbed by Doar's meritocracy, a fact that might have been both a symptom and a cause of Doar's regard for her. In either case, he seemed to have more confidence in her than in most of the other rookie lawyers on the staff, occasionally calling her in for private meetings to bounce ideas off her. But just as Doar took to Rodham, so, too, did Cates. She shared many of Cates's frustrations with the slow pace of the investigation. "This thing is going down in flames!" Tom Bell remembered Rodham saying one day when one of the president's men was acquitted of perjury charges vaguely related to Watergate. She was "devastated with the verdict," according to Bell, fearful that things were moving so slowly that Nixon and his men might prevail in the courts and in Congress. Bell, who felt that his job was to be loyal to Doar, urged Rodham to be patient. He said to her, "This is how lawyers work."

Bell came from Doar's law firm in New Richmond, Wisconsin, and shared his boss's moderate politics. He said that he and Rodham both "saw Nixon as evil," but in different ways. "Her opinion of him was more a result of the McGovern campaign and Vietnam and those kinds of issues. I saw him as evil because he was screwing with the Constitution. She came at it with more preconceived ideas than I did," Bell recalled. Their perspectives on Nixon paralleled to some extent the way in which the two young lawyers viewed their assignments. "She saw the work as absolutely the most important thing in the world," Bell said. "I saw it as important, but also as a job. To her it may have been more of a mission." The more Bell got to know Rodham, the more it became

apparent to him that "she wasn't as ideologically pure as the program for the players would indicate. Not that she made any false
pretenses or anything. We were just two young lawyers who
shared confidences." Their conversations were blunt and open.
"She wasn't afraid to say that you were full of shit. And if you told
her the same, she would take it."

Any doubt that members of the inquiry staff had about
Nixon's impeachability was removed when they put on headphones and listened to the White House tapes that they had obtained from the Watergate grand jury in late March. They spent
one week playing and replaying the tapes at the side of former
White House counsel John Dean, who had been present at many
of the meetings with Nixon where the cover-up was discussed.
Dean now served as an expert translator of the disjointed and
sometimes barely audible conversations that had been secretly
taped. The tapes immediately became the central focus of the
inquiry. Doar stored them in a safe in his office and assigned
Michael Conway, a classmate of Rodham and Clinton at Yale Law,
to serve as gatekeeper controlling access to them. He brought in
audio specialists to enhance the sound and held a competition to
determine which staff members had the sharpest ears and could
make the most sense of the conversations and accurately tran-
scribe them. A special listening room was set up at the end of the
hallway, not far from where Rodham and Bell worked.

Staff members would file in, turn on the tape machine, put on
headphones, turn off the lights, settle in on the couch and listen
to the president and his men. Rodham did not have the sharpest
ears on the staff, but she was in the room occasionally. She spent
several hours listening to what they called "The Tape of Tapes" —
Nixon taping himself while listening to his tapes, inventing ratio-
nales for what he said. At one point, he is heard asking Manuel
Sanchez, his valet, "Don't you think I meant this when I said
that?" Along with Fred Altshuler, another young lawyer on the
staff, Rodham also worked on a sophisticated organization chart
for the Nixon White House. By listening to the tapes and studying
the presidential logs that listed the people Nixon met with each
day, they reconstructed the daily decision-making process inside
the Oval Office—who had access to the president, how decisions
were communicated up and down. They developed case histories
for various events: if Nixon meets with Haldeman and Haldeman

talks about that meeting to Chuck Colson, what happens? Studying how the organization functioned, Altshuler said, "was important in terms of finding out whether the president in fact made decisions or underlings made decisions. If the chain of events is, X sees the president and comes out and does Y, you can draw an inference. We found that the president really ran an awful lot of details."

The end came quickly. In historic sessions at the end of July, the Judiciary Committee voted for three articles of impeachment. Within two weeks, the president had resigned. The inquiry staff was still at work that day, preparing documents for the full House debate on impeachment. They gathered in the library and watched Nixon's farewell speech on an old black-and-white television set. People sat on the floor and leaned against the wall and the sides of desks. The room was somber and quiet. No cheers from Rodham or anyone else. "It was like a game that ended in overtime — sudden death," recalled Michael Conway.

As a remembrance of their unforgettable time together, Doar gave each member of his staff a framed picture of the group on the front steps of the Longworth House Office Building. It was, like so many snapshots of Hillary Rodham, a reflection of her will. Before the picture was taken, Doar had instructed the lawyers to stand together in the front. Rodham had defied his request, calling it elitist. She stood in the back with her women friends on the support staff. Doar signed each picture with an inscription from the last quatrain of Tennyson's "Ulysses": "To Strive, to Seek, to Find and not to Yield."

From 1974 to 1998: then, Hillary analyzed the White House organization charts to determine the flow of the president's cover-up directives; now, Starr's deputies were analyzing detailed maps of the White House to determine who could have seen the president having sex with an intern. Then, Nixon went over a tape with his servant to try to put the best light on a cover-up conversation. Now, Clinton was going over a conversation he had with his secretary to try to put the best light on the reason they asked for some presents back from Monica Lewinsky. Watergate and Whitewater are vastly different in magnitude, yet it is nonetheless impossible to examine the forces that shaped the lives of Clinton and Rodham in 1974, and think about the forces that surround them now, and not be struck by the irony.

FOURTEEN

I know that my public comments and my silence about this matter gave a false impression. I misled people.

GAVE A FALSE IMPRESSION. Misled. President Clinton could not simply say that he had lied, which is what he did that day last winter during a White House event when he set his jaw, narrowed his eyes, wagged his finger, and declared that he "did not have sexual relations with that woman—Miss Lewinsky." A solid majority of Americans, according to opinion polls, said they assumed he was lying all along and did not care. The president was protected in his lie by the common sense of sex and politics. An extramarital affair is in itself a duplicitous act, so it is expected that someone having an affair will lie about it. Clinton in that way was just being human.

It is also a common assumption, supported by history, that politicians tell lies large and small as a means of survival. Kennedy lied to the public about Cuba, Johnson about Vietnam, Nixon about Watergate, Carter, who promised never to lie, about the aborted hostage recovery effort in Iran, Reagan and Bush about their knowledge of Iran-Contra. Lies in the political world come with rationalizations. In foreign policy, lies sometimes save lives (though they also often cost lives). There is a fine line between breaking a promise and telling a lie. Circumstances change. People mistake intent for fact, or hear what they want to hear, not what the politician says.

The August 17 speech was extraordinary in one sense: it marked the first time that Bill Clinton had acknowledged in public that he had purposely misled people. That admission, however grudgingly given, would unavoidably shade everything he said from then on. But it was far from the first time that people had suspected him of lying to them. In this case, as in so many previous instances, his evasiveness had the deepest impact on friends, not adversaries, and in most previous cases, those friends ended up forgiving him. When I heard him utter the "false impression" phrase in his speech, I thought back to one of the first interviews I had conducted in Arkansas during the early days of the 1992 campaign, with the state AFL-CIO president, J. Bill Becker. Nearly a decade after the fact, Becker was still sore at Clinton for what he felt was the most duplicitous behavior he had ever encountered in his career. It happened in 1983, when Clinton, after a two-year, voter-imposed hiatus, returned to the Arkansas governor's office, determined to make a national name for himself on the issue of the day, education reform.

Clinton decided to fund his education reform package by raising the state sales tax 1 percent. It was the least progressive form of taxation, unpopular with organized labor and advocates for the poor, but it was also the surest way to get the money he needed to raise teacher salaries and impose mandatory standards for all the state's schools, which ranked above only Mississippi's in test scores, teacher salaries, course offerings, and overall funding. In the legislative endgame, Clinton struck a deal with Becker and other social activists, who insisted on an amendment to the sales tax increase providing an annual rebate to low-income families for the sales tax on food. If they would lobby in the House for an emergency clause allowing the increase to take effect immediately, Clinton said, he would support their amendment. The deal was witnessed by two legislators, one of whom interrupted Clinton and repeated the terms to make sure the governor understood precisely what he was saying. Clinton said yes.

The House then passed the tax measure with the rebate amendment, but the emergency clause allowing it to take effect immediately failed by a narrow margin. The Clinton team got another shot at the same legislation the next day, and Becker and the rebate supporters, satisfied that Clinton was upholding his end of the bargain, joined forces again with the governor's aides, this time successfully pushing through the emergency clause. The next day, however, when leaders of the Senate said they had troubles with the rebate amendment, Clinton started backing away from that portion of the bill. By the time the Senate passed the legislation without the rebate for the poor and sent it back to the House for final action, Clinton and his aides were actively lobbying against the rebate. Clinton said it was his only choice to save the full reform package. Becker was enraged. He complained that Clinton had turned away from the rebate too hastily; the vote in the Senate would have been close, he agreed, but it might have passed with a strong lobbying effort by the governor.

During the time when he lobbied the House for the emergency clause as part of the deal, Becker said, several representatives had warned him, "Clinton's lying to you! He's lying to you! He's not going to do it." Becker had not believed them then, but later concluded they had been right. He had been active in Arkansas politics since the days of Governor Orval Faubus, he said, but never before had he felt so deceived by a governor. It was at the end of that episode that Becker uttered this verdict about the young governor: "Clinton will pat you on the back while he's pissing down your leg."

It was just politics, of course, part of the daily give-and-take of a Machiavellian world in which Clinton excelled. The teachers felt misled that same year. They had helped Clinton and his wife, Hillary, who headed the education task force, put together the reform package, only to find out that the Clintons had added a last-minute surprise—teacher competence tests. Cora McHenry, a field representative of the teachers' association and member of the task force, thought the competence test idea had been rejected until she heard about it on the radio as part of the final plan. What a surprise, what a betrayal, she remembered thinking. For three years after that, the teachers' union worked against Clinton, feeling that he had deceived them, but he finally won them back, and McHenry and other teachers were among his strongest supporters in 1992.

It was not untypical of Clinton that the only way he could run for president in 1992 was by overcoming an earlier act of deception. In preparing for his final race for governor in 1990, Clin-

ton had brought in several national consultants, including poll-
ster Stanley Greenberg and media specialist Frank Greer. He had
recruited them with the implicit understanding that the governor's race would be a prelude to a presidential bid. In recruiting
Greer, Clinton had said, "You always wanted me to run for president, but let me tell you, if I lose this race for governor, I'll never
get elected dogcatcher."

But not long after Greer signed on, Clinton attended a debate at which he was asked whether he would serve out his full
four-year term as governor if he won the election.

"You bet," Clinton said.

Did he mean it? Greer "died a thousand deaths," thinking
perhaps that Clinton had. But he did not mean it. The answer was
misleading, leaving a false impression. Clinton intended to run
for president if he could in 1992, but had been advised by several
friends in the National Governors Association that it would be
smarter for him to run as a sitting governor rather than as a former
governor. "You bet" was a convenient way for him to survive the
debate, and the governor's race, without immediately being revealed as a political opportunist.

That has apparently been a concern of Clinton's, and one of
the causes of his lies, since the beginning of his political career.
The lies he told about the way he manipulated his way out of the
military draft were meant to shield himself from charges of gross
opportunism. So, in a lesser way, was the story he told about how
he happened to come back to Arkansas to teach law in the fall of
1973. It was harmless, perhaps, but peculiarly Clintonian and revealing.

The way Clinton would tell the story for years afterward, his
hiring as an assistant professor at the University of Arkansas School
of Law that fall was "a pure accident." The phrasing is reminiscent
of his claim that his avoidance of the draft during the Vietnam
War was "a fluke"—which it certainly was not, no more than his
arrival at the law school was an accident. In the tale as Clinton
would tell it, he was driving home from Connecticut at the end of
his Yale days and, acting on a tip from a friendly professor,
stopped at a telephone booth along Interstate 40, placed a call to
the law school dean, and talked his way into an interview and a
job—simple as that, just a spur-of-the-moment bit of roadside
serendipity. Wylie H. Davis, the law school dean at the time,

would encounter the Clinton version of events years later and find it "amusingly inaccurate and somewhat melodramatic." And he would ask, "Why degrade a Horatio Alger–type story with a self-inflicted nuisance like the facts?"—to which he could only answer that he felt compelled by "neurotic lawyers and history buffs" to set the record straight.

The truth was that Clinton began aggressively pursuing a teaching position at Arkansas several months before he got his law degree at Yale. He recruited a political friend from Fayetteville, Steve Smith, to serve as his intermediary. Smith was a liberal young state legislator who had become friendly with Clinton during the McGovern campaign, when he was the only Arkansas delegate at Miami Beach to vote for McGovern on the first ballot. He talked about Clinton to J. Steven Clark, an associate dean at the law school who was also part of the state's political network. In March 1973, during his spring break from Yale, Clinton contacted Davis, the dean, who later recalled that from that point "the entire process was as deliberate and formalized as it was— and had to be—in every new hire case." The law school received glowing letters of recommendation for Clinton from several professors at Yale, as well as a record of his grades, which Davis and his colleagues paid little attention to because they found the Yale grading system "a slightly arrogant and eccentric neo-British affectation"—a deliciously cutting but misdirected insult, since the pass-fail system then in place at Yale Law was the product not of haughty academics but of rebellious students.

Clinton flew to Fayetteville in early May to appear before the Faculty Appointments Committee. David Newbern, who chaired the committee, had a curious first impression of the young applicant from Yale. On the morning of Clinton's first day in town, Newbern stopped at the Holiday Inn to pick up Clinton and escort him to the law school for a day of interviews. He encountered Clinton in the coffee shop talking to Steve Smith. Newbern wondered how Clinton knew Smith and why he would be engaged in such an intense political conversation on the morning when he was interviewing to become a law teacher. Later, he escorted Clinton from one faculty office to another. Finally, in an exit interview, Newbern asked the question that had been troubling him all day.

"Bill, are you coming to Arkansas to teach with us, are you

coming because you want to be a law professor, or is this just a stepping stone?"

"I have no plans at this time to run for public office," Clinton said.

It was, Newbern thought, the classic political response. In fact, Clinton was already planning the race for Congress he would make the following year, but he thought it would compromise his chances if he acknowledged that the law school job was part of a larger plan. The lie he told about how he came to Arkansas, the mythological story that it all happened by accident, served the purpose of softening the edge of his razor-sharp ambition.

Many of Clinton's lies come without evil intentions; that is, they are not aimed at doing harm to others so much as trying to present himself in a better light. This is one area where many of those who are the most self-righteous in denouncing him for lying might be more malicious than he is, spreading wild rumors about him that they do not know to be true. Spreading a false rumor is somehow not considered as dishonest as lying.

FIFTEEN

[I misled people.] Including even my wife. I deeply regret that.

I can only tell you I was motivated by many factors. First, by a desire to protect myself from the embarrassment of my own conduct. I was also very concerned about protecting my family.

To MANY OBSERVERS, the most puzzling statement in Clinton's entire speech was the regret that he had misled his wife. It seemed not so surprising that he would mislead her, but that she could be misled. Clinton's sexual behavior has been an issue in their relationship since before they were married. She has dealt with it time and again, sometimes privately, sometimes in front of the entire nation. Could it be possible that she did not know the truth about the Lewinsky affair? Did she not want to know? Those two questions can best be considered as part of the larger questions that have interested me since I began studying Rodham and Clinton for the biography: What keeps this uncommon partnership together? Why does she stay with him?

The first key to understanding Hillary's behavior today can be found in the original nature of her relationship with Bill Clinton. From the time they began dating at Yale Law School in 1970, they shared a passion for politics, policy, power, books, ideas — and they realized, they told friends, that they could attain heights together that they might not reach separately. He said that Hillary was the one woman he could see growing old with. He once told Melanne Verveer, whom he had known since his college days at Georgetown, that he was emulating Phil Verveer, Melanne's husband, in going for "brains and ability rather than glamour." He meant it as a compliment. For her part, Hillary's feelings about Clinton seemed more traditionally romantic. One friend described her as "besotted."

She was attracted not only by Clinton's wit and sense of purpose, but also by his demeanor. He was that rare guy, she told friends, who did not seem afraid of her. It might have been that he was more adept at concealing his fear. Rodham's intellect, her reputation, her refusal to be cowed or wowed, attracted him and scared him at the same time. He knew that he had to be at his sharpest when she was around. He lived then with three Yale classmates in a shambling house overlooking Fort Trumbull Beach on Long Island Sound, and he prepped his housemates before each of Rodham's visits, hoping that they could help impress her. It took a little time before "she decided that he was going to be up to snuff," recalled Don Pogue, one of the housemates. "She had to be encouraged to see that point of view. She was brought out to the beach house to engage in lively conversation. We were all recruited to participate in it."

Rodham expressed mixed feelings about Clinton's style, especially the way he accentuated his Arkansas roots. Like so many contemporaries who had encountered him before, she was taken by his sense of place, a rarity among students eager to shed their homogenized middle-class pasts, like hers in the bland suburban Chicago community of Park Ridge. If "A" for Arkansas was then his scarlet letter, he wore it with pride. "He cared deeply about where he came from, which was unusual," she told me once. "He was rooted and most of us were disconnected." But she was not bamboozled by his down-home palaver. "They were funny together, very lively. Hillary would not take any of Bill's soft stories, his southern-boy stuff," according to Pogue. "She would just puncture it, even while showing a real affection. She'd say, 'Spit it out, Clinton!' or 'Get to the point, will you, Bill!' " Another housemate, Doug Eakeley, who had been a Rhodes scholar with Clinton at Oxford, remembered Rodham, in her sharp voice, interrupting Clinton in the middle of one of his Arkansas tales with the mocking reprimand, "Come off it, Bill!"

Her midwestern directness, Eakeley thought, was "the perfect counterpoint to Bill's southern charm." Her focused intellect was also the perfect counterpoint to his restless, diffuse mind and made her the superior law student. In one class they took together during the spring semester of 1971, Tom Emerson's "Political and Civil Rights," Emerson kept private numerical grades even though the report cards were pass-fail. He gave Rodham a 78, one of the highest grades, and Clinton a less impressive 70.

There was, without stretching the point, a certain reversal of gender stereotypes in the Clinton-Rodham match. Steve Cohen, who was among Rodham's circle of friends, concluded that "Clinton had the charm and the sex appeal whereas Hillary didn't so much. Hillary was straightforward, articulate, and self-possessed." Yet within a month of meeting Clinton, she was talking about his depth. Some of her friends thought Clinton was interesting but too eager to be the focus of attention. Rodham decided there was more to him than that. "There's lots of layers to him," she told Cohen one day. "He's more complex than I thought. The more I see him, the more I discover new things about him." She also told friends about his determination to do something with his life, which was very much what she was about as well.

She seemed imbued from the start with a belief that Clinton was destined for greatness. During the Watergate summer, when she was working as a junior lawyer on the impeachment inquiry staff, she occasionally punched her office mate, Tom Bell, in the arm and proclaimed, "Tom Bell, Bill Clinton is going to be president of the United States someday!" Few took her boast seriously. Her East Coast friends were stunned when, two weeks after Nixon's resignation, she packed her suitcases in the trunk, strapped her bicycle to the roof, and climbed into friend Sara Ehrman's car for the long ride from Washington to Fayetteville to start a new life with Clinton. What would she find in Arkansas? they asked her. Why would she give up the high-powered legal and political career she could establish on her own to teach law in the Ozark hills? Ehrman, her landlady in Washington and friend from the McGovern campaign, tried to talk her out of the move even as they drove through Virginia and Tennessee.

"You are crazy," Ehrman said. "What are you doing this for?" Rodham laughed, said she loved Bill Clinton and wanted to take a chance.

From the moment she arrived in Fayetteville, there were signs of the problems that would plague them through the years. Clinton was in the middle of the congressional campaign against Hammerschmidt then, traveling around northwest Arkansas, and he had girlfriends in several towns. One of his campaign aides went into a tailspin when Clinton stole his girlfriend away from him. The suspicion around the campaign was that Hillary had dispatched her father and brother down from suburban Chicago to work as campaign volunteers in part to make sure Clinton behaved when she was not around.

Clinton once told Betsey Wright that he had tried to "run Hillary off" during that period "but she just wouldn't go." The young couple's loud arguments were unforgettable. "They'd have the biggest damn fights," recalled Ron Addington, a Clinton aide in the congressional race. "They had two or three battle royals." One day, Addington was driving Clinton and Rodham to an event in Eureka Springs, Clinton riding in front, Rodham in back, when the couple got into a furious argument over a campaign issue. Clinton was pounding on the dashboard, Hillary was hitting the seat, both were yelling. When they reached a stoplight, Hillary screamed, "I'm getting out!" and slammed the door behind her, walking all the way back to headquarters.

But it also seemed that they enjoyed mixing it up. As she later confided to a family friend, she could not imagine getting stuck in a boring relationship where there was no friction and energy. Before their marriage in October 1975, Hillary entered into intense discussions with friends on the question of whether a woman could establish her own identity and independent life within a marriage. Her model, she told friend Ann Henry, was Eleanor Roosevelt. Henry had just finished reading a biography of the first lady and offered Rodham a note of caution, pointing out that Eleanor never slept with her husband again after discovering that he was having an affair. "Eleanor never found her voice until that marriage was over," Henry added. "Until she didn't care about the marriage."

The second key to understanding Hillary's behavior in the Lewinsky scandal comes from the pattern that developed after she and Clinton got married, moved to Little Rock, and became the most powerful couple in Arkansas. Throughout that period from the late 1970s to the early 1990s, there were regular intervals when their personal relationship seemed endangered, often by Clinton's sexual behavior. The true extent of his infidelity is known only to him. He has acknowledged it to the degree of confessing that his actions caused "problems" in the marriage and that he was unable to meet a standard of perfection. In his deposition in the Paula Jones sexual harassment case, he also acknowledged having one sexual encounter with Gennifer Flowers, an allegation that he had vehemently denied when it threatened his nascent presidential campaign in 1992.

Flowers has said that her affair with Clinton lasted twelve years. She taped many of her telephone conversations with him in 1990 and 1991 when he was worried about a lawsuit filed against him by Larry Nichols, a disgruntled state employee, who named several women, including Flowers, with whom Clinton was alleged to have had affairs. The Flowers tapes were largely ignored when she released portions of them six years ago. They serve now as a peculiarly matched set with the tapes that Linda Tripp made of her discussions with Monica Lewinsky, the tapes that first roused the interest of the independent counsel's office in Clinton's sex life. In one of Clinton's discussions with Flowers after the 1990 election, they talked about the lawsuit and about how his opponent in that election, Republican Sheffield Nelson, was trying to stir up rumors about his sex life. "I stuck it up their ass," Clinton boasted on the tape. "Nelson called afterwards, you know." He said that Nelson had claimed that he had nothing to do with the infidelity allegations. "I know he lied. I just wanted to make his asshole pucker," Clinton said to Flowers. "But I covered you. . . ."

Clinton told Flowers that when Associated Press reporter Bill Simmons had first called him and read him the list of women he was said to have had affairs with, his initial response was "God . . . I kinda hate to deny that!" He had good taste, Clinton said. Then he added, "I told you a couple of years ago, one time when I came to see you, that I had retired. And I'm now glad I have because they scoured the waterfront." One of the other names on the Nichols list was Elizabeth Ward, a former Miss America from Arkansas. At the time, Ward denied that she had had an affair with Clinton. She changed her account after the Lewinsky story broke, saying that she had sex with Clinton once in the mid-1980s after he had romanced her in the back of his limousine.

According to friends of the Clintons, there was occasional mention of divorce, but it was never seriously considered. Clinton discreetly broached the subject twice with colleagues during meetings of the National Governors Association, and Hillary told friends that she thought about it during a rough stretch in 1989, when Clinton's infidelity seemed to go beyond sex and it was thought that he had fallen in love with another woman. According to Betsey Wright, then Clinton's chief of staff, Hillary concluded that she had invested too much in her marriage and was determined to see it through. Even in the toughest moments, it was not apparent that their emotional bond had broken. Wright described it as "an intensely argumentative but passionate" relationship, though there were times when Hillary was mad enough to stop talking and give Clinton the cold shoulder for weeks.

But the most important pattern that developed over the long haul in Arkansas was that in times of real crisis, when Clinton's career, and their shared dream, seemed imperiled—for whatever reason, his personal behavior or larger political forces—it was Hillary who took the lead and made it possible for him to survive and recover. She did this largely by coolly focusing her energy outward, transforming their personal trauma into a larger cause. This habitual response intensified their symbiotic relationship at moments of vulnerability and made it easier for her to repeat the process the next time.

The defining crisis of this sort came in 1980, when Clinton, defeated after a single two-year term as governor, was rendered at age thirty-four the perfect symbol of the sardonic definition of a Rhodes scholar: a bright young man with a great future behind him. Clinton was depressed by the loss, consumed by bitterness, convinced that journalists had conspired against him, doubtful that he could recover. Hillary stepped in and made recovery possible. She summoned Dick Morris and Betsey Wright to Little Rock to launch the comeback. She went to the press and calmly described the forces that were at work against her husband, explaining that he had lost because "there was no effective counterattack" to the negative stories spread by his opponent, Frank White, and the Republican right. She identified key journalists who had turned against Clinton and went out and flattered them in lunch meetings and over the telephone.

And she set about changing her own image as well. Since

Clinton's first race for governor in 1978, his opponents had tried
to make something out of the fact that she went by Hillary Rodham, her maiden name. It was very un-Arkansan, they would im-
ply, marking Rodham as an outsider who stubbornly resisted the
mores of her adopted state. This sentiment was shared by many of
Clinton's friends, including his own mother. During the 1980
campaign, one powerful member of the Arkansas House offered
the opinion to a Clinton ally that "Hillary's gonna have to change
her name and shave her legs." Rodham had ignored the issue
then, but after his defeat, with her and her husband's political ambitions on the line, she reconsidered.

Her change, in typical Rodham fashion, was more intellectual than emotional. When a friend dropped by the Clinton
house the morning after a party in Little Rock, Rodham asked her
a question that the friend had never heard from her before: "What
are people wearing?" It was clear that Rodham was making the
transformation from studied feminist, keying in on the fact that
her name was political, as was her appearance. Years later, when
asked by New Yorker reporter Connie Bruck about the name
change, Clinton recalled a conversation he had had with his wife
in which she approached him and said, "We've got to talk about
this name deal." As Clinton remembered it, Rodham told him
that she did not want him to lose an election because of her last
name. When Clinton protested, she placed the decision in the
most pragmatic political terms: "We shouldn't run the risk. What
if it's one percent of the vote? What if it's two percent?"

She colored her hair, bought contacts and abandoned her
thick-lens glasses, compiled a new wardrobe, used more makeup,
and changed her name. No more Hillary Rodham in public; now
she was Mrs. Clinton. This complete makeover was not the un-
characteristic sacrifice that many later made it out to be. Hillary
had always had an ability to play different roles at different times.
As malleable as Bill Clinton often seems, his personality in many
ways has always been more set than Hillary's. In a letter she wrote
during her college years at Wellesley, she talked about intention-
ally assuming different roles, now the social activist, now "sticking
to the books," and occasionally "adopting a kind of party mode."
She claimed that she even got outrageous at times, but immediately modified that assessment—"as outrageous as a moral Meth-

odist can get." In her search for identity, she thought of herself as "a progressive, an ethical Christian and a political activist."

For those who later watched and judged Hillary Clinton's behavior as the wife of a presidential candidate and then first lady—here asserting her maiden name, there relinquishing it; here deferring to her husband, there telling him what to do; here posing like a model for the cover of traditional women's magazines, there emphasizing substance over style; here searching for the moral meaning in life, there playing the commodities market to make a quick buck; here disparaging cookie-baking housewives, there peddling her chocolate chip cookie recipe; here saying that she was not some Tammy Wynette standing by her man, there doing exactly that, time and again, from Gennifer Flowers to Monica Lewinsky—it is instructive to know that she was, self-consciously, always this way.

In any case, at the low point in Clinton's life, Hillary did whatever she thought was needed to bring him back, and it was a pattern that she followed from then on. Throughout his final decade as governor, even as their marriage went through a series of tests, their professional partnership grew ever stronger. From the ashes of the 1980 defeat, she emerged as his key policy adviser and political strategist. Clinton came to have an implicit faith that whatever she did for him would turn out right, that whenever he got himself in trouble, she would bail him out. The pattern was disrupted only once, in 1994, when he placed her in charge of the national health-care issue and for a variety of reasons, some her doing, others not, the effort failed miserably. The health-care disaster not only robbed the Clintons of their best chance to have a landmark legislative legacy, it not only became a major reason why the Democrats lost control of Congress, but it also again rearranged the Clinton & Clinton partnership. The president became less politically dependent on Hillary than at any time since 1980— until, that is, he needed her again when the Lewinsky story erupted.

In the first days after the story broke, some of the central questions of the Lewinsky drama again concerned the first lady: What would she do, and why would she do it? Would this be one sex story too many for her to tolerate? Would she recede from public view in a state of depression, or would she take the lead on her husband's behalf? Many of those questions were posed in subdued tones inside the White House itself, where aides, expressing anxiety and confusion, said they were looking for her to ease their minds and give them a sense of direction in contrast to the president's ambiguity.

In keeping with her long-established pattern, she moved steadily to resolve the questions, or at least smother them, responding as she had in earlier times of crisis. She seized control of her husband's defense with the outwardly unfazed certitude of a battle-tested veteran. She brought back the old friends, political lawyers Mickey Kantor, Harold E. Ickes, and Susan Thomases, and also the Hollywood image maker Harry Thomason. She said what she thought needed to be said about her husband. She loved him. People misunderstood him. She believed him. She went on NBC's *Today* show and reconstructed the scene in which her husband told her about the sexual allegations as though he were a bewildered Ozzie Nelson awakening Harriet from slumber, as though she were an ordinary wife, trying to live an ordinary life, her sleep interrupted by the inanities of the outside world. ("You're not going to believe this, but . . ." Clinton began, rousing Hillary in the middle of the night of January 21. "What is this?" she asked quietly. ". . . but I want to tell you what's in the newspapers," he continued.)

Seven months later, here was Clinton on national television, confessing to an improper relationship with Lewinsky and saying that what he regretted most of all was misleading his wife. Was it possible? The fact that Hillary established the defense in this case, as she had so many times in the past, does not mean that she and her husband always had frank discussions about the details of his indiscretions. In both the Paula Jones and Lewinsky cases, according to several sources, Clinton shared his innermost concerns with his lawyers more than with Hillary. There was, despite all that they have been through, or perhaps because of it, a degree of "Don't ask, don't tell" in their partnership. Her habit has been to defend him publicly no matter what; and his habit has been to realize that she would do so, making it less urgent for him to tell her everything. Considering the nature of their relationship over the course of a quarter-century, the notion that she might leave her husband in January, when the story broke, or in August, when he confessed, seemed almost beside the point. If she left, she would in effect be leaving herself.

SIXTEEN

PRESIDENT CLINTON'S HISTORY suggests two other reasons why he misled everyone for seven months: he was trying to figure out the questions on the test, and he was waiting for luck.

It is in Clinton's nature to think of the difficulties he gets into as a series of final exams. Some people become anxious and lose their bearings before a test; Clinton's reaction is usually the opposite. He is the ingenious but nonchalant student who always excels at taking tests. As an undergraduate at Georgetown, he studied the whims and inclinations of his professors, flattered them, emulated them, and by the end of the semester could predict what questions they would ask on finals. At Yale Law School, he could skip class for months, borrow a friend's notes for eleventh-hour cramming, and still score higher than the dutiful note taker, even if it appeared that he had spent more of the night before reading Proust than civil procedure.

It was that second characteristic—Clinton as the carefree quiz whiz—that allowed him to maintain a relatively calm public persona during the weeks leading up to his August 17 date with the grand jury and speech to the nation. But the first talent, his uncanny ability to predict questions on any exam, was more tenuous than at any time in his life. Unlike a droll professor from Clinton's college days, Proctor Starr had not been susceptible to flattery, and he had refused White House requests that the president be apprised of the line of questioning beforehand. Clinton, the natural politician, had always shown an insatiable hunger for information about the people and the environments in which he operated, constantly plying aides, friends, acquaintances, even strangers, with his trademark question: *Whadaya hear?*

Circumstances had forced him now to change that style. The president who once chafed at the confinements of his job by calling the White House "the crown jewel in the American penal system" was confronted with the prisoner's paradox: an existence in which he was rarely by himself and yet always alone. Many associates had been afraid to talk to him for fear of being subpoenaed. The president told one friend that he had worked out much of his thinking late at night while playing solitaire. His daily study group had been reduced to his lawyers. While they tried to construct an approximation of the prosecution's case, they did not know the full universe of evidence amassed on the other side, what could or could not be refuted.

The grave danger of not knowing all the questions had been brought home to the president on the January day that he was deposed in the Paula Jones sexual harassment lawsuit. "Now," said one of Jones's lawyers to the president, "do you know a woman named Monica Lewinsky?" And so began a round of fifty questions on a subject that Clinton had not fully anticipated. He knew that Lewinsky's name had been on a list of potential witnesses in the Jones case, but he did not know that the Jones lawyers had been tipped off to Linda Tripp's tape recordings of Lewinsky talking about her relationship with Clinton. Those moments in the deposition room, said one former White House lawyer, "had to be among the most frightening of Bill Clinton's career—all he could have been thinking was 'How did this happen?' and 'I can never let this happen again!'"

It was with that in mind that he delayed as long as possible before feeling compelled to testify before the grand jury. And one reason why he modified his story and acknowledged an inappropriate relationship with Lewinsky was that he remained, even after seven months, unable to figure out the test, to intuit the least obvious questions on Starr's master list.

During many of the personal and political crises of his life, Clinton has also followed a pattern of waiting until luck comes his way, which seems to happen quite often. It is not blind luck, but an instinctive sense of timing combined with manipulated luck, what baseball's Branch Rickey called "the residue of design."

The most obvious example was during the late 1960s, when he was dealing with the military draft and was in the predicament of opposing the war in Vietnam, not wanting to serve in the military, but also not wanting to be considered a draft dodger. He dragged out his decision for as long as possible, delaying one induction date, joining the ROTC and then backing out of that agreement when the first draft lottery came around and he drew a lucky number, 311, so high that he would never be called.

In politics, his providence has taken a different form. At several critical points when his career seemed threatened, he had been lucky about who his adversaries were and skillful at forcing them to overplay their hands against him. The latest and most significant instance came late in 1995, when the Republicans in Congress handed him back his faltering presidency, along with a second term, by shutting down the government—an act that Clinton in essence goaded them into, and that made them appear reckless and allowed him to remodel himself as the moderate voice of reason. Clinton and his strategists this time had hoped that Starr would fall into the same trap and provide the president with a lucky escape once again. In a political sense, this happened. Starr's public ratings plummeted when he aligned himself with right-wing judges and financiers, and appeared to be obsessive in his pursuit of Clinton in the Lewinsky matter. He was as unpopular as Newt Gingrich ever was, but the difference was that it did not matter, he could keep going, because he was protected by the independent counsel laws and not subject to public sentiment.

SEVENTEEN

The fact that these questions were being asked in a politically inspired lawsuit which has since been dismissed was a consideration too.

In addition, I had real and serious concerns about an independent counsel investigation that began with private business dealings twenty years ago—dealings, I might add, about which an independent federal agency found no evidence of any wrongdoing by me or my wife over two years ago.

The independent counsel investigation moved on to my staff and friends. Then into my private life. And now the investigation itself is under investigation. This has gone on too long, cost too much, and hurt too many innocent people.

WAS THIS AN APOLOGY? Here is where the speech turned, midway through the seventh paragraph, and Clinton took the offensive. White House aides who had worked on early drafts had offered Clinton words that would make him sound contrite, not peeved, and they groaned as they watched him launch his attack. Orrin Hatch, after demanding repentance, reacted with the stunned disbelief of a parent whose child had refused to obey, declaring that he was ready to blow his stack and that Clinton was "a jerk." As I watched Clinton make this sudden turn, it seemed to me the most predictable element in his speech. It was the almost inevitable result of a personality that explained and rationalized compulsively; that tended ever to the political strategy of attacking his attackers, believing that everything is political and that politics is war; and that relied on a partnership with a wife who believed that even more than he did. The belief that his adversaries had once again gone too far provided Clinton with a justification for his counterattack.

The need to rationalize was always there with Clinton, going back to his childhood, but the reflexive attacking of the attackers was something that he acquired during his political education.

After his sophomore year at Georgetown, Clinton went back to Arkansas to work in the 1966 gubernatorial primary campaign of Judge Frank Holt, a moderate Democrat from Little Rock. Holt was a solid, reliable, gentle man, and became a father figure of sorts to young Clinton. He was also the constant target of attack from his opponents, who said that he was too closely aligned to the old machine of Orval Faubus. Jim Johnson, whose race-based demagoguery made him the Arkansas equivalent of George Wallace, said that Holt was "hand-picked by the big boys" and was nothing more than "a pleasant vegetable." Another candidate said that Holt was a passenger on the "Faubus steamroller" driven by the retiring governor's political enforcer, William J. Smith, who was said to wield the sort of raw power that made legislators straighten up a little when he came into view. If the supposed links to Faubus were not enough, reporters were tipped off that Holt had met privately with the state's most powerful financier, bond broker Witt Stephens, only hours before entering the race, implying that he was Stephens's puppet as well. Rumors spread that he had been promised a federal judgeship if he lost.

These broadsides against Holt were for the most part bogus. Although he arose from the party establishment, he was not beholden to Faubus or Stephens, but suffered from his own becalmed temperament. He demonstrated passion once, at the start of the campaign, when he paid his filing fee, banged his fist on the desk, and bellowed, "I am completely free and unobligated!" That done, he assumed naively that the attacks against him would end.

Clinton not only shared Holt's philosophy, he also thought that staying above the fray was the surest path to victory. In a letter to his college girlfriend, Denise Hyland, he wrote of Holt: "Denise, he's never lost an election and I see why. He really lives by his religious and ethical convictions without being self-righteous or pious. He refuses to attack his opponents as they attack him. He wants to win on his own merits or not at all. He thinks he can't build Arkansas unless he wins that way."

Holt lost the primary runoff to Jim Johnson, and Bill Clinton's campaign philosophy was never quite so pure again. By 1978, when he was running for governor himself in an easy race, he and his newly hired consultant, Dick Morris, spent much of their time plotting strategy for another contest, a U.S. Senate primary between David Pryor and Jim Guy Tucker. Clinton wanted Pryor to win that primary because he considered Tucker, who was young and handsome and moderate, his main competition as the rising star of Arkansas Democratic politics. According to Morris, Clinton became concerned that Pryor "was being too nice a guy and wasn't aggressive enough in the campaign," so he spent hours devising negative themes that Pryor could use in ads against Tucker.

But it was not until Clinton lost the 1980 gubernatorial race to Republican Frank White that the concept of attacking the attackers became a habitual part of his political makeup. Clinton blamed everybody but himself for that loss: President Carter, for bringing Cuban refugees to Fort Chaffee, where they rioted; journalists, for questioning his first-term actions and raising the notion that he was more interested in his national reputation than his performance in the state; he even blamed the voters for failing to appreciate why he had raised the car tax to pay for better roads. But in the end what he mostly blamed the loss on was his underestimation of his conservative adversaries and his hesitance to declare war on the opposition. He defined his new tactic in a speech at a Democratic party workshop in Iowa in 1981: "When someone is beating you over the head with a hammer, don't sit there and take it," he said. "Take out a meat cleaver and cut off their hand."

This tactic fit in perfectly with what Morris began preaching to him in 1983 once he returned to the governor's office. Clinton's problem, Morris said, was that he had bisected means and ends with "an almost Catholic splitting of virtue and sin." Candidate Clinton would do what it took to get elected, but Governor Clinton would "go about serving without any significant thought to the political connotations, with almost a shunning of that which would be politically useful." Means and ends had to be "completely interwoven," Morris said, into what would become known as the permanent campaign. From then on, Clinton governed as he campaigned: trying to go over the heads of the media directly to the people, constantly polling to find out the best way to shape his rhetoric, and responding quickly and strongly to the slightest attack. In Arkansas, Clinton and his aides eventually mastered the art not just of selling him to the public but also of diminishing the attacks against him through effective damage control.

This helped Clinton reach the White House, but it also created an atmosphere that poisoned and endangered his stay there. Everything was viewed in political terms, including legitimate questions about his governance or investigations into his behavior. During the 1992 presidential campaign, the Clinton War Room in Little Rock, headed by aides James Carville and George Stephanopoulos, was celebrated for its adeptness at damage control, and Clinton and his aides took the War Room mentality with them to Washington, making little or no distinction between what it meant to run for president and what it meant to run the country. It was the failure to understand that distinction that led Clinton to hold fund-raising teas in the Oval Office and to offer overnight stays in the Lincoln Bedroom to major contributors. And also, finally, to take steps to limit the damage of sexual allegations against him that Kenneth Starr and the prosecutors believe might constitute obstruction of justice, but which to Clinton were merely standard operating procedure in his permanent campaign.

Bill and Hillary Clinton have long felt that they engendered hatred in their adversaries that exceeded the norm, that people spread false rumors about them, that there was, as Hillary claimed in her famous *Today* interview with Matt Lauer last January, "a vast right-wing conspiracy" out to destroy Clinton. This perception seems to be an odd combination of the real and the conveniently imagined.

From that first congressional campaign in 1974, it became apparent that Clinton evoked a visceral hatred in some people, who would then say anything they could dredge up to disparage him. In that race, conservative preachers denounced him from their pulpits, calling him a homosexual or a libertine or both.

They said that his campaign headquarters was a drug haven. Rumors spread that he was the "Boy in the Tree," a longhaired protester photographed holding a banner in a tree during President Nixon's 1969 appearance at an Arkansas Razorbacks football game. Most of the allegations were false, the last one absurdly so—Clinton was at Oxford at the time of Nixon's visit.

I have often been asked to explain the depths of this animosity toward Clinton, and though I know the history of it, my answers have never fully satisfied me. Many of the reasons appear obvious. Some people hate his politics. Others think he is a phony, a liar, always getting away with something, and it drives them to distraction. Others are infuriated by the way he tries to co-opt their worlds. Some on the religious right cannot stand the fact that Clinton is a Southern Baptist who can quote Scripture as well as they can. Some Republicans get infuriated by the way he takes traditionally Republican issues like welfare reform and makes them his own.

There has always been a generational aspect to it, a feeling among some that Clinton epitomized the white, middle-class, well-educated, liberal baby boomers who did not have to struggle in life, avoided the Vietnam War and other difficult tests, and after great moralizing in their younger days, when they disparaged the sacrifices of their elders, lapsed into hypocritical adult lives defined by ambition and self-centeredness. It is a harsh generalization, and the stereotype does not fit Clinton exactly, but it has been applied to him nonetheless, and every example of his ambition, selfishness, or hypocrisy is held as evidence of a generation's failures. But the odd thing about this sentiment is that it is held most strongly by Clinton's own cohorts, male baby boomers, while members of his parents' generation are more likely to forgive his erring ways, especially his sexual promiscuity, and look only at his words and his policies.

In any case, Clinton and his wife chose to interpret the intense dislike for them as purely political and largely conspiratorial. Hillary was the key theoretician in the family in this regard. Because there always seemed to be an element of exaggeration in the claims against Clinton, it became possible for her to lump everything together and dismiss it as the imaginings of their enemies. On conservative talk shows, in videotapes sponsored by Jerry Falwell, in a newspaper funded by right-wing financier Richard

Mellon Scaife, in all of those venues at one time or another, Clinton had been accused of every evil act imaginable: murdering Vince Foster, killing as many as a dozen people in Arkansas, conspiring with the CIA and drug runners. Where did the zealotry of Clinton's enemies end and the truth begin? It is one of the many ironies of the Clinton tragedy that he was always his worst enemy, while his enemies, by overreacting, were often, unwittingly, his strongest allies.

At times, Clinton emphasized the conspiracy theme with Hillary as a means of preparing her for more allegations coming his way. Near the end of *The Agenda*, Bob Woodward's book on the first two years of Clinton's first term, just as the Whitewater investigation is getting under way, Hillary reflects on what she sees as the "politically motivated attacks aimed at undermining" her husband's presidency. She remembers a telephone call that her husband told her about back in 1991, just when he was "pumping up" to run for president. The call was from someone in the Bush administration who had worked with Clinton on state policy issues, and as Hillary recalled her husband telling her the message, it went like this: "We've done a lot of looking at this race and your profile as a candidate is one, and one of a very few, that could cause us trouble. And we just want you to know if you get into this race, we will do everything we can to destroy you personally."

Who made the call? Hillary declined to say at first, but eventually she and Clinton passed word through an aide that it was Roger B. Porter, Bush's domestic policy adviser. Porter, a mild-mannered policy wonk, said he had no such conversation with Clinton and was not aware of anyone else in the Bush White House who knew Clinton well enough to say such a thing. In the only conversation he had with Clinton in 1991, Porter said, he told Clinton that he ought to switch to the Republican party if he wanted to become president.

Clinton's telling of that tale to Hillary served another purpose: it provided her a means from then on of transforming her personal trauma into a political cause. Gennifer Flowers, Paula Jones, Monica Lewinsky—all received by her in the same way, not as evidence of her husband's irresponsibility, but as signs that people were out to get them. She spent considerable time in early 1994 holding off-the-record discussions with editors and opinion leaders in Washington during which she presented her conspiracy theories. Those presentations were not unlike what she said on national television in January: "The great story here, for anybody willing to find it and write it and explain it, is this vast right-wing conspiracy that has been conspiring against my husband since the day he announced for president."

In the four days before Clinton's August 17 speech, word seeped out day by day that he was preparing to change his story and acknowledge an improper sexual relationship with Lewinsky. It was clear to me then, given their history, that the only way Clinton could proceed with that change of course was with Hillary's agreement, which meant that he would have to tell her in more detail about his relationship with Lewinsky. Whether Hillary could have been as surprised and devastated by his confession as friends and aides, including the ubiquitous Jesse Jackson, made it seem is questionable. But it seemed predictable, based on the patterns of their relationship, that she would have the strongest voice in the final shape of his speech, and that it would not be simply a confession, but another assertion of will against their perceived enemies, a brief in his defense. As one of her aides once said about Hillary: "She's a litigator. Every day she gets up and goes to court. When she loses, she files an appeal."

EIGHTEEN

*Now this matter is between me, the two people I
love most, my wife and our daughter, and our
God. I must put it right. And I am prepared to do
whatever it takes to do so.*

 *Nothing is more important to me personally,
but it is private. And I intend to reclaim my family
life for my family. It's nobody's business but ours.
Even presidents have private lives. It is time to stop
the pursuit of personal destruction and the prying
into private lives and get on with our national life.*

IT HAS COME FULL CIRCLE; this is where it all began, I thought to
myself as I heard Clinton utter those words. Go back eleven years,
to the summer of 1987, when Clinton was first about to run for
president, only to be talked out of it at the last minute. The issue
then was the same as now: Clinton, his behavior, his wife and
daughter, and the line between private and public lives.

 In the months after Gary Hart dropped out of the race early
that May, and Clinton's name surfaced as a possible late entry into
the presidential primary field, the question lingered: Did Bill
Clinton have a Gary Hart problem?

 As journalists and party activists in Washington asked the
question among themselves, and in so doing advanced Clinton's
reputation as a womanizer, Clinton and his friends and advisers

struggled with how to deal with it. Bob Armstrong, the former Texas land commissioner who had developed an easygoing, big-brotherly friendship with Clinton since they worked together in the McGovern campaign, had several telephone conversations with Clinton in the aftermath of the Hart implosion. One of the issues Clinton brought up, according to Armstrong, was whether there was a "statute of limitations on infidelity—whether you get any credit for getting it back together." Armstrong told Clinton that he thought not. Clinton and Betsey Wright also had several private debates over the lessons of Hart's demise. Clinton "wanted to believe and advocated that it was irrelevant to whether the guy could be a good president," Wright recalled. She argued that it had a significant bearing in Hart's case because "it raised questions about his stability." Any previous affairs might have been irrelevant, she said, but "to have one while he was running was foolhardy."

Clinton agreed. Hart, he said, was foolish to flaunt it.

Dick Morris was also brought into the discussions, even though by then he was working almost exclusively for Republican politicians. Clinton questioned Morris at length about how he thought the public would react to the infidelity issue and whether it would be held against him. They gingerly explored different ways to address the topic or sidestep it. Morris sensed that Clinton had "a tremendous terror of the race because of the personal scandals that were visited upon candidates who ran. His experience watching candidates be destroyed by those scandals or impaired by them chilled him, and led him to a feeling that this was a terribly inhospitable environment in which to tread." The sex issue, Morris said, "loomed large in his consideration. It loomed very large."

But the momentum kept building for Clinton to run. In July, his friends around the nation were called and urged to come down to Little Rock for the announcement. A ballroom was rented at the Excelsior Hotel for July 15. A few days before the scheduled announcement, Betsey Wright confronted Clinton one last time with the issue of extramarital sex. She listed the names of women he had allegedly had affairs with and the places where they were said to have occurred. "Now," she concluded, "I want you to tell me the truth about every one." She went over the list twice with Clinton, the second time trying to determine whether any of the women might tell their stories to the press. At the end of the process, she suggested that he should not get into the race. He owed it to Hillary and Chelsea not to, she said.

The next day, Wright drove to the airport and picked up Carl Wagner, the first of a group of Clinton friends who had planned to gather in Little Rock for the presidential announcement. Wagner was a generational cohort who had met Clinton in Washington during the antiwar organizing in the summer of 1970. They had gone through the McGovern campaign together, Wagner running Michigan while Clinton ran Texas, and had kept in touch ever since. Wagner, like Clinton, loved to talk on the phone. Clinton had asked him to come down to Little Rock a day early to help "think this thing through." Wright did not tell Wagner about her encounter with Clinton the day before.

Wagner met with Clinton and Hillary at the Governor's Mansion that night. They sat around the table in the kitchen and talked for several hours. It was an intense conversation in which Wagner and Hillary assessed the practicality of Clinton making the race, element by element. Wagner noticed that Clinton was more comfortable talking about policy, depersonalizing the discussion. He wondered whether Clinton was prepared for the consequences if he became a candidate. At the end of the evening, as Clinton and Hillary moved toward the stairs leading from the kitchen up to their second-floor bedroom, Clinton turned to Wagner, who was still seated at the table, and asked, "So what's the bottom line?"

"I tell you what," Wagner responded. "When you reach the top of the steps, walk into your daughter's bedroom, look at her, and understand that if you do this, your relationship with her will never be the same. . . ."

By early afternoon the next day, a dozen Clinton friends from around the country had congregated at the Governor's Mansion for an announcement-eve luncheon. Most waited in the living room as Clinton sat on the porch steps leading out to the back lawn, engaged in a final conversation with Wagner and Mickey Kantor, a California lawyer and Democratic activist who had been part of Clinton's network since the Carter era. If Clinton had privately made up his mind after his encounter with Betsey Wright, if he had reached a decision after the discussion with Wagner in the kitchen the night before, he still felt a need to weigh the options to the last possible moment. As the three men talked, Chelsea, then seven years old, approached her father and asked him about a family vacation planned for later that summer. Clinton told her that he might not be able to go because he might be running for president. "Well," Chelsea said, "then Mom and I will go without you."

Chelsea always had a powerful effect on Clinton. She was perhaps the one person in the world whom he unconditionally loved. The subtext of his relationship with his daughter was his own unfortunate history with fathers. He did not want to be considered a neglectful father himself, yet his political obsession gave him little time with Chelsea. He tried to soften the guilt by joking about it, often telling the story of how when Chelsea was asked at school to describe what her father did, she had said, "He gives speeches, drinks coffee, and talks on the telephone." As true as it was amusing.

Clinton decided not to run, and in the statement he issued that evening, he centered his thoughts on Chelsea: "I've seen a lot of kids grow up under these pressures and a long, long time ago I made a promise to myself that if I was ever lucky enough to have a child, she would never grow up wondering who her father was."

Four years later, Clinton was ready to run. He had talked it out with Hillary and they had agreed that the race was worth it; together they could handle whatever stories were thrown at them. In early September 1991, on the eve of what he and Hillary expected to be a difficult interrogation concerning his sex life, Clinton met again with a few close advisers to discuss how he should answer indelicate questions. The very notion that he would have to talk about his private life infuriated him; he argued that it was hypocritical and irrelevant, and that if he were divorced no one would care at all. Finally, it was agreed that he would offer a modified confession along these lines: There had been some problems, but he and his wife had worked through their troubles and were committed to the marriage.

With the response seemingly decided upon, Clinton took a break from the strategy meeting and went to dinner in Georgetown with an old friend. A few hours later, he returned and said, "Hell, I just had dinner with Vernon Jordan and Jordan said, 'Screw 'em! Don't tell 'em anything!'"

Fragments of those scenes from 1987 and 1991 came back to

me as I listened to Clinton declare that he intended to reclaim his family, that nothing was more important to him than Hillary and Chelsea, that this was nobody's business but theirs. I thought of Mickey Kantor, who had witnessed that scene with Chelsea when she was seven, and who now found himself as one of the president's private counsels, the man who carried around the yellow notepad pages containing Clinton's backward-looped cursive first draft of his ill-received apology. And of Vernon Jordan, who had told Clinton back at the dawn of his first presidential race to screw 'em all and not say a word about his sex life, and who now stood as one of the central figures in the whole Lewinsky mess. And of Chelsea, whose parents had been telling her since she was a little girl that her daddy's enemies would say nasty things about him, and who had now heard from him directly that he had had a relationship with a woman nearly as young as she was.

NINETEEN

THE PRESIDENT ALSO TURNED TO GOD in this part of his speech, a moment I had been anticipating. "Our God," he said, a phrase meant to underscore the fact that both he and his wife would turn to faith to help them through another crisis. The night before, in the White House residence, he had prayed with Reverend Jackson from Psalm 51: "Have mercy on me, O God . . . and cleanse me from my sin." I have always been intrigued by the interplay between the spiritual lives of the Clintons and their personal and political lives, and the manner in which they bathe themselves in religion during troubled times. Coming out of vastly different religious cultures, Hillary, the United Methodist, and Bill, the Southern Baptist, both found that religion eased the burden of their high-profile personae, sometimes offering solace and escape from the contentious world of politics and the private stresses brought on by Clinton's behavior, other times providing theological support for their personal actions and political choices.

During their Arkansas years, Hillary Clinton seemed to fit her religion and her Church so well that one of her ministers called her "a model of Methodism." She, in fact, took much of her political inspiration from the founder of Methodism, John Wesley, an eighteenth-century Anglican priest who mixed social reform with evangelical piety. "As a member of the British Parliament, he spoke out for the poor at a time when their lives were being transformed by far-reaching industrial and economic changes," she said in a speech explaining why she was a Methodist. "He preached a gospel of social justice, demanding as determinedly as ever that society do right by all its people. But he also preached a gospel of personal responsibility, asking every man and woman to take responsibility for their own lives."

In her speeches on Methodism, Hillary always recited her favorite exhortation from Wesley: "Do all the good you can, by all the means you can, in all the ways you can, in all the places you can, at all the times you can, to all the people you can, as long as you ever can." Yet at the core of her belief, thought one of her ministers at United Methodist, the Reverend Ed Matthews, was a personal need as strong as or stronger than the social commitment. "One of her favorite thoughts," Matthews told me, "was that the goal of life is to restore what has been lost, to find oneness with God, and until we find this we are lonely."

As her and her husband's troubles increased during their years in the White House, Hillary embarked on an ever greater search for "what has been lost." She sought guidance from New Age spiritualists and carried religious readings in her purse, turning to them at night or alone in her hotel room on the road. Her favorite reading was from the writings of Catholic theologian Henri Nouwen, about the parable of the prodigal son and "the discipline of gratitude," a phrase that she said she thought about during her most trying times.

For Bill Clinton, the prodigal son, religion offered something other than discipline and gratitude and social service. Many clues to the way he has responded to the Lewinsky scandal can be found in his religious history. He began attending church when he was nine years old, toting a leather-bound Bible in his left hand as he walked alone down the streets of Hot Springs, past the motel swimming pools and nightspot parking lots, the corridor of middle-American carefree vacation glitz, to Park Place Baptist Church. The pastor, the Reverend Dexter Blevins, said that young Clinton was at the church not just Sunday mornings but "every time the door opened," and seemed starving for a refuge from the inner turmoil of his family life. "It was an important part of my life," Clinton told me in 1992. "It was moral instruction . . . trying to get closer to being a good person and understanding what life was all about. I really looked forward to it every Sunday morning, getting dressed up and walking that mile or so alone."

During his years in Little Rock, his church was Immanuel Baptist, an imposing, rectangular shrine of gold and tan that occupied two full city blocks, standing alone on a hill at Tenth and Bishop, looming above the state capitol and the workday world of the city. It was one of the largest churches in Arkansas, with more than four thousand members and a statewide television audience for the live broadcasts of the eleven o'clock Sunday services — another effective means for Clinton to reach his electorate. He was a second tenor in the church choir, and though he never had time for choir practice, on Sundays he "would get up there and act as though he had rehearsed the whole thing," recalled Mary Francis Vaught, the minister's wife. "He would sing as big as anything."

Dr. W. O. Vaught, the leader of Immanuel Baptist, became Clinton's father figure until his death in 1989. They seemed an unlikely pair. Vaught was everything Clinton was not: short, bald, bespectacled, stern-voiced, reliable, a conservative religious scholar. He was an intellectual storyteller, translating the Old and New Testaments from Hebrew and Greek and giving his worshipers detailed syntactical and semantic explications of the text. Through those interpretations, Vaught had a profound effect on Clinton's thinking on several important social issues of the day, most notably the death penalty and abortion. In seeking spiritual justification for imposing the death penalty, Clinton leaned on Vaught's interpretation of the Ten Commandments in ancient Hebrew and Greek. The original phrase, Vaught taught him, was "Thou shalt not murder," not "Thou shalt not kill" — which he said meant it did not preclude states from following the law and imposing capital punishment. On abortion, Vaught again turned to a semantic reading of ancient works, arguing that the meaning of life and birth and personhood came from words that in ancient Hebrew literally meant "to breathe life into." From that, he concluded that the literal meaning of life in the Bible would be that it began at birth, with the first intake of breath. That did not mean that abortion was right, Vaught told Clinton, but he did not think one could say it was murder.

Whether Vaught and Clinton ever discussed the precise biblical definition of sexual relations is unknown. But it is apparent that during the Lewinsky affair, when Clinton tried to make the argument that oral sex was not sex, he was again, as usual, drawing on his history, and he was basing it not so much on his legal training as on the biblical semantics that he first learned from his Little Rock minister.

TWENTY

Our country has been distracted by this matter for
too long, and I take responsibility for my part in all
of this. That is all I can do. Now it is time, in fact
it is past time, to move on. We have important
work to do, real opportunities to seize, real prob-
lems to solve, real security matters to face.

And so tonight I ask you to turn away from
the spectacle of the past seven months, to repair
the fabric of our national discourse and to return
our attention to all the challenges and all the
promise of the next American century. Thank you
for watching and good night.

THE THEME SONG of Clinton's first presidential campaign was
Fleetwood Mac's "Don't Stop (Thinking About Tomorrow)"—
and never was a candidate attached to a more appropriate an-
them. Clinton's entire life has been a rush to tomorrow, away
from yesterday and today. In his undergraduate years at Georgetown, he was influenced heavily by a professor of Western civilization named Carroll Quigley, one of whose favorite themes was
the notion of future preference. He argued that what made America great was the willingness of each generation to sacrifice for the
next. "One thing will kill our civilization and our way of life,"
Quigley told his students, "and that is when people no longer

have the will to undergo the pain required to prefer the future to the present." Over the ensuing decades, Clinton rarely delivered a major political speech that did not include a paraphrase of that lecture.

As a political idea, future preference has always been a winner. Americans are optimists who believe that their futures will be better than their pasts. Many of Clinton's strongest policies, especially his support of education and civil rights, are built on the notion of future preference, and it is that theme, in my opinion, that showed the glimpse of potential greatness in him. But to Clinton, future preference became more than that; it gave him, when in distorted form, the final defining aspect of his self-deluding character. Blocking out, denying difficult truths, creating his own sense of reality, compartmentalizing his life, using semantic nuances to explain his behavior, relying on his wife and aides to protect him—and finally, always, pushing the past and the present away, moving on to the future, to what's next. When an aide went in to brief him on a subject or an upcoming event, Clinton's habit was to keep doing some other activity, reading or writing, at the same time he was being briefed. Every half-minute or so, without looking at the aide, he would say, "What else?"—not as a question, but as a sign that he had catalogued the information and it was time to move on. These were the words Clinton came to live by: *What else? What else? What else?*

Clinton once told me that he was haunted by W. J. Blythe's early death. Knowing that his father had died young made Clinton rush through life in a hurry, he said. "Because I grew up sort of subconsciously on his timetable, I never knew how much time I would have. It gave me an urgent sense to do everything I could in life as quickly as I could." Every year or so when he was in Arkansas, he would drive down to Hope and visit the gravesite at Rose Hill Cemetery, where his grandfather James Eldridge Cassidy and father, William Jefferson Blythe, were buried side by side. Blythe died at twenty-eight, Cassidy at fifty-six. When he gazed at their tombstones, Clinton said, he became "acutely aware that you never know how much time you have." Once, after stopping at the graveyard, Clinton wrote a letter to a friend saying that the visit was "a good reminder that I have a lot of living to do for two other fine fellows who never even got close to the average life span. . . . If I die tomorrow I guess I'd feel in a way that I've lived a long time—and a full time. But should I live to be old I know I'll feel as if I just started on this journey of life and hardly be ready to leave." The one book Clinton took on his honeymoon was a brilliant work by the philosopher Ernest Becker titled *The Denial of Death.*

TWENTY-ONE

No ONE in the political world liked Clinton's speech. Dee Dee Myers, his former press secretary, watching from the set of CNN's Larry King show in Washington, said it was "mostly downhill" from the moment her old boss said his introductory "Good evening"—and that about summed up the general attitude. His words had failed him. More than that of any politician in modern times, Clinton's career has been defined by a debate over his words: what he has said, or hasn't said, or almost said, or denied saying, or insisted that he had said, or people thought he had said. The stakes in that debate over his words seemed to increase every year, until finally they reached the level of whether his words constituted perjury or obstruction of justice.

Clinton was a natural-born talker, rarely exact or eloquent, but loose and rambling and inventive and colloquial. Now and then, in extemporaneous situations, usually late at night when he could feel the passion of a crowd, he found the rhythm and poetry of a great country orator and sent a room into a spell of awed silence. But those speeches were always about optimism and persistence and hope and common ground, about being there for the people until the last dog died. Everything in his history allows him to give that speech. The hardest speech for him would be the one in which he had to say that he killed the dog—and that is what many people wanted to hear on the night of August 17.

It is part of the circular irony of Bill Clinton that the most memorable speech of his presidency might be one that lasted only four and a half minutes and that people listened to word-for-word and that failed miserably. It was ten years earlier that he had first entered the national consciousness by giving a televised speech that lasted more than half an hour and that nobody cared about or wanted to listen to and that also failed miserably.

On the night of July 20, 1988, Clinton strode to the platform at the Democratic convention in Atlanta to the theme of *Chariots of Fire* and declared, "I'm honored to be here tonight to nominate my friend Michael Dukakis for president of the United States"— and as Dee Dee Myers would say, it was all downhill from there. Clinton's wife and aides and friends looked on in horror as he droned on and on, the house lights on, delegates chanting and yammering. ABC cut away at the twenty-one-minute mark and began showing a film. On NBC, Tom Brokaw uttered forlornly, "We have to be here, too," and then gave up on the speech. CBS showed a red light flashing on the podium, a signal for Clinton to shut up, then found a delegate in the audience giving Clinton the cut sign with a hand slash across the throat. And people could be heard shouting, "Get the hook! Get the hook!"

The morning after was unforgiving. On NBC's *Today*, the studio host asked correspondent Tom Pettit how Clinton could have been described as "someone to watch" on the national scene. "Now we know better," deadpanned Pettit.

Two terms as president later. Everything different, everything the same—that is the way it is with Bill Clinton. It took him several days to realize how much he had muffed it this time. Day by day, after the speech, as he worked the telephones and listened to friends and associates, he slowly began accepting a little more of the blame for what he had done. He knew the patterns of recovery—he had done it so many times before—but this was unlike any of his other crises, and it remained uncertain whether anything he said or did could help. The press seemed determined to get a better apology out of him, drip by drip.

When he visited Russia in early September, he insisted that he had meant his speech to be an apology. In Northern Ireland, he finally uttered the word *sorry*. More refinements came until finally, on September 9, in his most complete statements of contrition, he told Democrats in Congress and party faithful in Florida that he had understood that he had let everyone down—them, his family, the country—and was determined "never to let anything like that happen again." It was fitting that Clinton began making the apology that people wanted to hear on the same day that his nemesis, Kenneth Starr, finally sent his 453-page report on the Lewinsky affair to Congress along with thirty-six sealed boxes of grand jury material, what Starr called "substantial and credible" evidence that may warrant the president's impeachment. The crucial battle had begun.

The Starr report revealed little new beyond the explicit details of a pathetic White House dalliance—four years and $40 million to establish, conclusively, what the world already knew: that Bill Clinton was sexually reckless and that he would go to great lengths to try to conceal his behavior from family, aides, friends, party, enemies, and the voting public. On the day of the report's publication, Clinton apologized yet again, this time hitting the notes that many had been listening to hear for three weeks: he called himself a sinner and said that at last he had hit the "rock-bottom truth."

But from my perspective as his biographer, the true ending to the speech that Clinton had begun on August 17 came on Friday, August 28, at Union Chapel in Oak Bluffs, Massachusetts, when he interrupted his Martha's Vineyard vacation to attend a ceremony honoring the thirty-fifth anniversary of Martin Luther King's "I Have a Dream" speech. This is how Clinton closed his remarks that day:

All of you know I'm having to become quite an expert in this business of asking for forgiveness. And I—It gets a little easier the more you do it. And if you have a family, an administration, a Congress, and a whole country to ask, you're going to get a lot of practice.

But I have to tell you that in these last days it has come home to me again, something I first learned as president, but it wasn't burned in my bones—and that is that in order to get it, you have to be willing to give it. And all of us—the anger, the resentment, the bitterness, the desire for recrimination against people you believe have wronged you—they harden the heart and deaden the spirit and lead to self-inflicted wounds.

And so it is important that we are able to forgive those we believe have wronged us, even as we ask for forgiveness from people we have wronged. And I learned that first—first—in the civil rights movement. "Love thy neighbor as thyself."

The reaction to those comments among media pundits was that Clinton had blown it again, and only confused matters, by saying that he had asked his administration, the Congress, and the whole country for forgiveness. When? He had not done it in the August 17 speech, nor any time since in public. True enough, but that was not what interested me. Nor was I particularly taken by his attempt to link his personal troubles to the civil rights movement. American politicians in trouble had been doing the same for years, and Clinton was just following that traditional practice, and doing it before a sympathetic audience. Nor was I surprised by the sense in those remarks that Clinton still felt that *he* had been wronged. What stuck with me was what he said about his bitterness and resentment: *they harden the heart and deaden the spirit and lead to self-inflicted wounds.*

I had always wondered about Clinton's inner life, what he said and thought only to himself, in his mind, at the end of the day. It is something that no biographer, no other human being, can ever know. When the public persona is immaterial, when the rationalizations do not work, when there is nothing to compartmentalize, when there are no hands to shake or votes to be won, when the only thing interpreting your words is your own conscience, what then? A self-inflicted wound. A hardened heart. A deadened spirit. Did he realize how he had mortally damaged his own great promise? This brought back to me the time in 1992 when I had asked Clinton what his deepest moral challenge was, and he had responded, speaking about himself in the third person, that it was "the failures of daily life that often grind people down and leave them so disappointed with themselves." We were on his campaign plane that night, and after giving that answer he rose from the chair and ambled up the aisle to his seat at the front. A half-hour later, he returned with one final thought. He said that he forgot to mention that he and Hillary had been talking more in recent years about what it meant to live a good life and the nature of life after death.

Did he believe in life after death?

"Yeah, I have to," Bill Clinton said. "I need a second chance."

ACKNOWLEDGMENTS

IN ONE SENSE, this book came quickly. I wrote it in a short and intense burst between President Clinton's August 17 speech and the release of the Starr report on September 11. But in another sense it was the product of more than six years of work—the time I have spent researching, writing, and thinking about Bill Clinton in various ways: as an author for Simon & Schuster, as a television commentator for NBC, and most of all as a journalist for *The Washington Post*. As usual, my editors at the *Post* gave me a wonderful sense of freedom and community, and for that I thank Leonard Downie, Robert Kaiser, Steve Coll, Karen DeYoung, Bob Woodward, Bill Hamilton, Maralee Schwartz, and all my reporting colleagues. Whenever I was stumped in search of a date or fact, it was reassuring to know that Bobbye Pratt in the *Post* library was always there to help.

Although I grew up a mumbler and consider the written word my best form of communication, my experience in the world of television has helped me sharpen my thinking on Clinton, and for that I am grateful for the interviewing skills of Keith Olbermann, Tim Russert, Katie Couric, Matt Lauer, Chris Matthews, Brian Williams, Tom Brokaw, and their many producers and assistants.

The concept for this book came from Alice Mayhew, my editor at Simon & Schuster, who has been a wonderful source of ideas, energy, and enthusiasm in my writing career, as well as a tough competitor in croquet on her uneven Sag Harbor playing field. Thanks also to her assistant, Layla Hearth, to everyone else at Simon & Schuster, and to my agent, Rafe Sagalyn. My parents, Mary and Elliott Maraniss, might disagree with some of my conclusions about Clinton, but I have always considered them the voices of reason and good conscience against which I judge everything that I say and write. I could say or write nothing at all without the unending love, wisdom, and good humor of my wife, Linda, and our kids, Andrew and Sarah.